DETHRONING MAMMON

DETHRONING MAMMON

MAKING MONEY SERVE GRACE

The Archbishop of Canterbury's Lent Book 2017

Justin Welby

B L O O M S B U R Y

LONDON · OXFORD · NEW YORK · NEW DELHI · SYDNEY

Bloomsbury Continuum
An imprint of Bloomsbury Publishing Plc

50 Bedford Square
London
WC1B 3DP
UK

1385 Broadway
New York
NY 10018
USA

www.bloomsbury.com

Bloomsbury, Continuum and the Diana logo are trademarks of Bloomsbury Publishing Plc

First published 2016

British Library Cataloguing-in-Publication Data
A catalogue record for this book is available from the British Library.

ISBN: PB: 978-1-4729-2977-8
          EPUB: 978-1-4729-2978-5
          EPDF: 978-1-4729-2979-2

6 8 10 9 7

Printed and bound in Great Britain by CPI Group (UK) Ltd, Croydon CR0 4YY

MIX
Paper from
responsible sources
FSC® C020471

To find out more about our authors and books visit www.bloomsbury.com.
Here you will find extracts, author interviews, details of forthcoming events and
the option to sign up for our newsletters.

To Caroline

CONTENTS

FOREWORD

This is a beautiful and important book to accompany people as they walk through Lent towards the poverty of Jesus on the cross and his subsequent resurrection. Last Lent a young assistant with no religious faith living in L'Arche asked me, 'What is Lent all about?' I replied that it is a time where we think about all the poor and lonely people of the world, refugees and the elderly, prisoners and those controlled by addiction. It is a time for addressing the barriers that divide us from one another. 'That is a good idea,' he replied.

Perhaps the greatest divide today is between the poor and the rich. It is a great and terrible divide, so wide that those on either side cannot even imagine its breadth. Those of us who have cars, who easily afford a plane ticket, who frequently purchase new clothes and have our food shipped from many different continents to our plate, cannot imagine the lives of those who have none of that available to them. And yet, our decisions, our consumption, have resounding effects upon everyone on this planet.

And some of these effects are amounting to crises. Ecological destruction, religious extremism, violent political regimes – these all have some roots in greed and the impetus to have more and more and more.

So the question of Mammon is pressing. But what is it? In this little book, Archbishop Welby wisely dissects the defining characteristics of Mammon. They infiltrate our day-to-day lives with such subtle discretion that we may not even be aware of Mammon's pervasive presence. If we *are* aware, then every day, in little ways, we can immediately begin this urgent process of dethroning Mammon, of making room for Jesus.

In many ways, L'Arche, the community I have lived in for over half a century, is the antithesis of Mammon. My community, like nearly one hundred and fifty others in the world, is composed of men and women, with and without intellectual disabilities, living together. Part of our mission is to make known the gifts of people with an intellectual disability. But another profound vocation of L'Arche is to welcome young assistants who have often lived unquestioningly guided by Mammon, by competition and efficiency and productivity. That is the reality of our society today. In L'Arche, they discover something very different. Those who have no 'value' in society are the centre of our community. Our way of life together allows for the spontaneous, the creative, the inherently human to shine through. And competition quickly disintegrates into play and cooperation because each person is unique and gifted and beyond compare. Some have called L'Arche a school of the heart. What is true is that many of the lessons revealed in this book by Archbishop Welby are enacted (often unintentionally) in L'Arche. I would even go so far as to suggest that people with an intellectual disability have an amazing gift for 'dethroning Mammon'.

I greatly appreciate this book and the journey it leads us on through Lent. As I explained to that young assistant, Lent is a time of compassion, but it is especially a time of preparation and liberation. Some people give up sweets or coffee, a symbol of giving up what appears essential in our lives so that Jesus can once again become central. This book is also about liberation. It is about freeing ourselves from the principles and spirit that amount to Mammon, freeing ourselves to be true disciples of Jesus. Let us prepare together for that ultimate liberation which is Easter, Jesus resurrected and alive today.

Jean Vanier

June 2016

Introduction

Key text *Matthew 13:45-6*
The Parable of the Pearl of Great Value

Jesus Christ sets us free through obedience to him. Serving Christ is no slavery in the way we understand the term, but an entry into the most beautiful and glorious freedom. He does not use underhand means to gain power, but lures us into ever more beauty and purpose, ever-deeper relationships and self-realisation, simply by the power of his compelling and unconditional love.

But the more interconnected the world becomes, the more power is held over individuals and nations by economics, by money and flows of finance. Mammon – a name given by Jesus to this force – gains strength through our obedience. The more we let ourselves be governed by Mammon, the more power he[1] has, and the more the vulnerable suffer.

It is that extraordinary contrast, between Mammon and Christ, that has made me want to write this book. In so many human crises, money plays a part. Debt and desire for things enslaves many people I know, and draws them into lives that are in the service of Mammon, a master they neither choose nor want, but who tricks them by playing on insecurities, on good intentions and on reasonable ambitions. At a national and international level, every crisis seems to end in talk about economics – not economics as a tool in the service of human flourishing, but as an end in itself. It seems that in many eyes, and often in mine, personal finances that are in good shape, or a national or global economy doing well, are not merely a means to improve people's lives, but are seen as *the* goal in pursuit of a good life.

That approach is incompatible with serving Christ. It is incompatible, yet God, in grace and love and patience, meets us, blesses us, calls us and guides us, even while we are possessed by the power of Mammon. God waits for us to find the real treasure in life, and to begin the incredibly radical steps – the first steps in a journey that will last a lifetime – to bring us to the point of losing everything for the sake of the treasure of the Kingdom of Heaven.

MATTHEW 13:45-6

Again, the kingdom of heaven is like a merchant in search of fine pearls; [46]on finding one pearl of great value, he went and sold all that he had and bought it.

Jesus talks about the kingdom of heaven in numerous parables, and in Matthew 13 there is a great series of them. In vv. 45-6, we have the parable of the pearl of great price. It is a striking parable because it concerns a merchant, someone accustomed to doing good deals, someone that Jesus' hearers would have recognised as 'canny', as they say in northeast England. The merchant buys and sells pearls as a business, until one day he finds a pearl of pearls, more beautiful, more valuable than any other. He is entranced with it. He sells everything he has and buys it. The parable is very short indeed, but vivid in the extreme. One of the first rules of business is that one should never bet everything on one deal, but should hedge one's bets. Yet here is this clever businessman doing just that. We don't have any idea what comes next – what happens to the pearl – but now the merchant has it as his own. The image on the front of this book is a profound and striking depiction of this scene.

In some interpretations of the parable, the merchant represents the believer, who, after much seeking and finding of good things, finds that uniquely great thing, the kingdom of heaven. In Matthew's Gospel the phrase is used to convey the idea of the area of God's rule. We enter it only by surrendering to the King, Jesus himself. The merchant recognises that everything else he has held on to is worth nothing compared to this treasure, and that nothing is worth keeping if it stops him getting hold of the pearl of great value.

But the parable can be understood in another way; the merchant is God, who demonstrates that he will hold nothing back in order to claim that which is most precious. The pearl of great value represents you – and me – for whom God gives up his only Son in order that we may know ourselves as loved, claimed, belonging, 'held' close to God's heart as his most valued treasure.

In the shadow of the cross (as the cover painting so vividly depicts), we are urged to see ourselves as the pearl in God's hand; but also, at the same time, as merchants. This book seeks to explore a small proportion of those things that prevent us from following the example of the merchant. It suggests some ways in which we can tackle our own reluctance, and the pressures of our culture to conform us into being those who see the pearl, but fail to see it for what it truly is and thus hold on to lesser treasures instead.

In addition, I seek to explore some of the tensions that arise in our society because we are so dominated by economics and finance, the modern aliases of Mammon. It is very difficult to live well and with right attitudes in a society where the current prevailing values push us in a very different direction. There is much to be admired and valued in society today, especially in the United Kingdom. There is genuine valuing of people, profound security compared to many parts of the world, enormous wealth (even if its distribution is significantly unequal and exacerbated by rising house prices that benefit those at the top most), a commitment to universal health and welfare, and many other benefits and blessings besides.

I do not want to be grumpy or negative, or to hark back to some mythical golden age of Christian virtue. I am deeply thankful to have been born and raised here and now, in this age and at this time. Yet there is also much cause for concern – especially since the crash of 2008, often called the Great Recession. This is discussed more fully in Chapter 1. My concern springs from our turning away from the early and tentative questioning of the underlying ethical values of economics, and a resumption of the debt-fuelled, crisis-creating model that led us into such trouble in the past. Ethics have become (particularly in our political discourse) an economic enhancement, valued but not fundamental. In this book, I explore some of the underlying assumptions and suggest that economics, as an alias of Mammon, should also be subordinated to Christ, which means being controlled and led by an ethic that seeks human flourishing. This has been exemplified in the great system of Catholic Social Teaching as developed over the last 125 years.

Mammon, with ethics as an add-on rather than a foundation, calls the weak to suffer in the name of the general good. There is nothing new about such an attitude. In his *History of the Peloponnesian War* (a war of around 431–404 BC), Thucydides describes the Melian dialogue. Athens threatened to attack the Melians, offering them an alternative of humiliating surrender and effective serfdom. Against the Melian appeal to divine justice they said, 'The strong do what they have the power to do and the weak accept what they have to accept.' Such also is the impact of Mammon.

The quote is paraphrased in a recent book[2] in which the former Finance Minister of Greece, Yanis Varoufakis, argues that in good times the global system of economics deals with economic imbalances through market mechanisms, but that these only clear the imbalances when times are easy. When hard times come, heavy-handed institutional and self-protective responses crush the poor. Our world has seen this again and again at times of crisis, from the sovereign debt troubles of the 1980s, through the crash in the Far East in the late 1990s, most clearly in 2008, and in the terrible deflation and economic depression imposed on the poor of Southern Europe since 2009.

John Maynard Keynes was the architect of the Bretton Woods settlement that after the Second World War set up institutions to deal with the sort of crises that had been created by the Great Depression of 1929–32. Bretton Woods worked for many years, until the early 1970s, at which point global events could no longer be resolved by the assumptions on which the system had been built. Until then, it had reflected Keynes' understanding that economics was embedded in ethics[3], representing a vision for an economically and relationally functional world.

Drained by the terrors of world war, exhausted by the memories of the 1930s, appalled by the idea that such events might recur, the world powers of the late 1940s were willing to compromise economically – at least to a certain degree – for stability, justice and virtue.

Now we must find an approach to economic justice that works in fair weather and foul, but that will require brilliance, vision and political leadership. Another Keynes is needed. It is only within such a global system that it is possible for individuals, businesses and societies to dethrone Mammon, and to give all for the pearl of great price.

It would be absurd to write much here about the outcome of the 2016 referendum on the United Kingdom's membership of the European Union. At the time of writing (early July 2016), and I expect for some time to come, the long-term effects of the decision are impossible to predict or decipher.

Suffice to say three things: first, it is essential that the new United Kingdom outside Europe is not built to a design drawn by Mammon; to put it more clearly, materialism is not the answer to the challenges we face. Rather, we need a deep sense of the priority of the human person, whoever they are and wherever they come from.

Second, once again we remind ourselves that Mammon always deceives his followers. A campaign fought on his agenda will lead to division and even despair. To displace Mammon and dethrone his power involves an agenda of hope and love, rejecting the idea that we only value what we measure, or that we hang on to what we have, keeping it from others. Failure to reimagine our country with an agenda based on hope and love will lead to yet more disappointments.

Lastly, how we structure the way we relate must be led by values other than Mammon's. The renegotiation of our position in Europe, or elsewhere, as I hope this book helps to demonstrate, must be one that starts with the authority of Christ, not mere calculation of dubious material advantage.

The aim of this book is thus to encourage a Christ-directed questioning and examination of our attitudes to everything from our own wealth (or lack of it), through to a critical and prayerful approach to what is good at the level of local, national and global economics.

Why is such an aim appropriate for a Lent book? Because Mammon is so powerful that an attack on his authority over our lives, attitudes and thinking is as good a way of preparation for the reality of the Passion and crucifixion as I can imagine. Never mind chocolate, or even alcohol: try giving up materialism for Lent, and try reforming the way we understand what is good and bad in the economy. Put all of it into prayer, and find that, although the world won't change overnight, a revolution may begin, because God is the one who brings new life by raising Jesus Christ from the dead.

And what gives the Archbishop of Canterbury the authority to write about such things? This book is essentially a personal thinking-aloud, an attempt to answer a question I was asked in the mid-1980s by a curate at my church. Talking to me about Christians in the workplace when I was

Group Treasurer of Enterprise Oil, he asked, 'But what is a *Christian* treasurer that anyone else is not?' It is a question that is still with me.

How are Christians distinctive in their approach to money? In this book, I make some suggestions, which are not 'professional' answers – either theologically or economically – nor are they aimed at a specialist readership. Rather, they are an expression of my own ongoing journey of discipleship. Whether or not you agree with me, it will be good if my thinking aloud provokes deeper reflection.

The narrative of this Lent book starts before Holy Week, the week leading up to Good Friday, and ends long after it. Within each chapter, there are questions for reflection. Those who are interested may wish to use these as material in a study group for Lent. The writing and questions assume a Christian worldview, but I hope they are also accessible to those who aren't regular churchgoers.

Chapter 1 deals with our inbuilt tendency to value what we see. We look at one of Jesus' most significant miracles, the account of the resurrection of Lazarus in John 11, and how it enables his sisters to see the world through God's eyes. It calls for reflection on what we look for, and how we know it when we see it. The pearl merchant was searching, and when he saw a pearl of great value he knew what it was, and what he needed to do in response. Are we able to become like him?

Chapter 2 turns from what we see to how we assess and measure things, and the impact of that on ourselves and those around us. Taking the events of Luke 19, as Jesus passes through Jericho on his way to Jerusalem and to the triumphal entry and the cleansing of the temple, I reflect on the danger of measuring, because how we measure shapes in important ways what we see. The merchant knows how to measure pearls, as well as how to look and what to see. False measurement would have led to commercial disaster for him, while right measurement led him to the pearl of greatest value.

Chapter 3 reflects on the question of an 'acquisitive' nature, of our very human and understandable tendency to hold on to what we have, to say that what is ours is truly ours, not truly God's, and act accordingly. We return to Lazarus' home in John 12, and the extravagance of Mary's anointing of Jesus' feet in order that he might be glorified. The merchant had to lose all that he already had in order to acquire the pearl. Holding on to what he had would have prevented him from acquiring what was infinitely better. In Chapter 3, moving us towards the second half of the book, I begin to ask about how we might overcome such a tendency to hold on.

Chapter 4 looks at the links between power and money, and at the way in which we settle into thinking that what we have gained is by our own efforts rather than through the grace of God. As a result we have a wrong attitude to possession, and cling to power that protects wealth. In John 13 Jesus washes the feet of his disciples. The recovery of a sense of grace as the origin of all things opens the way to humble service, the common good, and the love for one another that dethrones Mammon.

Chapter 5 arrives at the burial of Jesus, and the actions described in John 19 of two of his lesser known followers, Joseph of Arimathea and Nicodemus. In this chapter, there is a much longer section which looks at the prevailing assumptions about the way economies work and what matters in them, aiming to make us more self-aware about the invisible but powerful influences on our attitudes to money and possessions. Awareness of what shapes our thinking enables us to ensure that our influence is Christ, not Mammon.

Chapter 6 goes to the end of all things, again looking at issues of money and value, and recalling some of the themes of the first three chapters. Looking at the letter to the Laodiceans in Revelation 3 and the fall of Babylon in Revelation 18, it asks us to take a perspective on money that begins and ends with Christ. It speaks of the deep impact of false seeing, but also of the immeasurable love of Christ that meets each and all of us in our lostness, and offers hope, purpose and a future.

What we see we value

Key text *John 11*
The Death of Lazarus

No experience of suffering or sorrow is able to overcome the capacity of God to bring life. The generosity of God overflows with such power that even death is swept away. But the power of death to deceive, to cause us to see wrongly the nature and purpose of our existence in this world, is something we all experience at some point. When we are at the funeral of a loved friend or relative, we hear death saying to us, 'I am the final answer. All ends in this complete nothingness and emptiness. Do not deceive yourselves.'

What we see we value. In our society, we value wealth that is visible, and life that is confident. Those being interviewed for jobs lose marks for being quiet, and not putting what they have on show. The flashy and confident are likely to be promoted, despite the fact that they often prove disappointing. We listen more carefully to, and are often taken in by, someone who is 'successful', with evident wealth. We airbrush out those in sickness, despair, depression and want. Such conditions speak more of absence and death – on which we prefer not to dwell – than prosperity and growth, and so we tend to value them less.

Christians should see more clearly, because we have seen Jesus. We are people whose vision has been challenged and corrected, so that we can see the world as it properly is. But seeing badly is still a big problem for most of us most of the time; when we see God and the world wrongly, the problem becomes an issue of great menace.

Jesus spent much of his ministry sorting out the mis-seeing of others. The resurrection was the biggest sight-correction of all, but before that there were several moments of immense force and drama in which Jesus challenged the way we see things.

The raising of Lazarus was one such moment. In John's account of the story of the Passion, the raising of Lazarus comes just days before what we now call Holy Week, the week leading up to Jesus' own dying and rising. This is a time of huge tension, with Jesus moving resolutely towards Jerusalem, and finding himself in furious confrontations with the rulers. Behind the scenes, they are planning to kill him, and are seeking to find a disciple who can be persuaded to betray him.

JOHN 11:1-16

Now a certain man was ill, Lazarus of Bethany, the village of Mary and her sister Martha. ²Mary was the one who anointed the Lord with perfume and wiped his feet with her hair; her brother Lazarus was ill. ³So the sisters sent a message to Jesus, 'Lord, he whom you love is ill.' ⁴But when Jesus heard it, he said, 'This illness does not lead to death; rather it is for God's glory, so that the Son of God may be glorified through it.' ⁵Accordingly, though Jesus loved Martha and her sister and Lazarus, ⁶after having heard that Lazarus was ill, he stayed two days longer in the place where he was.

⁷Then after this he said to the disciples, 'Let us go to Judea again.' ⁸The disciples said to him, 'Rabbi, the Jews were just now trying to stone you, and are you going there again?' ⁹Jesus answered, 'Are there not twelve hours of daylight? Those who walk during the day do not stumble, because they see the light of this world. ¹⁰But those who walk at night stumble, because the light is not in them.' ¹¹After saying this, he told them, 'Our friend Lazarus has fallen asleep, but I am going there to awaken him.' ¹²The disciples said to him, 'Lord, if he has fallen asleep, he will be all right.' ¹³Jesus, however, had been speaking about his death, but they thought that he was referring merely to sleep. ¹⁴Then Jesus told them plainly, 'Lazarus is dead. ¹⁵For your sake I am glad I was not there, so that you may believe. But let us go to him.' ¹⁶Thomas, who was called the Twin, said to his fellow disciples, 'Let us also go, that we may die with him.'

The raising of Lazarus was an event that divided its witnesses into separate camps according to what they thought they saw. In the story, we see different groups of people reacting in different ways to the same reality, and they do so because they viewed the same event through different eyes.

The Pharisees and the chief priests reacted to Jesus' miracle by deciding to have him put to death. The raising of Lazarus was the last straw. Though they, just like Mary and Martha, had just witnessed someone who was dead come back to life, they did not value the life of Lazarus, and so they did not truly *see* it. Instead, the authorities valued the political and economic stability of the Temple. What they really *saw* in the raising of Lazarus was a threat to the status quo, in the form of a revolutionary named Jesus. Even if their eyes witnessed a miracle, what they perceived was a threat.

Mary and Martha, at the beginning of this episode at least, see only through eyes of grief. What we see we value. They act according to the world they see, and what they see is death. The only certainty of this circumstance in their mind is that their brother is dead, and so they object to Jesus' talk of resurrection. They do not know that Jesus embodies a certainty even greater than death. Jesus challenges them to see with the eyes of faith that life in him is stronger than death.

What don't you see?
Which people do you ignore?
To which places do you turn a blind eye?
What reality do you pretend not to notice?

Seeing correctly is one of the greatest spiritual disciplines. We see much of competing value. Many things stand before us and claim to represent ultimate value or power. That is especially true of bereavement. All those who are bereaved know the sense of the power of death that carries someone off to a place where we cannot go. And yet Jesus tells us, through Mary and Martha, that what those two sisters saw, and what we all see, is an illusion. The reality is life everlasting.

Jesus sees perfectly. Amid remarkable pressure, Jesus is constantly maintaining peace, focusing on what is near, and is not distracted by anything. His deliberate steps towards Lazarus are remarkable because they show that he understood, by seeing into the situation more deeply than those around him, what needed to happen.

JOHN 11:17-27

When Jesus arrived, he found that Lazarus had already been in the tomb four days. [18]Now Bethany was near Jerusalem, some two miles away, [19]and many of the Jews had come to Martha and Mary to console them about their brother. [20]When Martha heard that Jesus was coming, she went and met him, while Mary stayed at home. [21]Martha said to Jesus, 'Lord, if you had been here, my brother would not have died. [22]But even now I know that God will give you whatever you ask of him.' [23]Jesus said to her, 'Your brother will rise again.' [24]Martha said to him, 'I know that he will rise again in the resurrection on the last day.' [25]Jesus said to her, 'I am the resurrection and the life. Those who believe in me, even though they die, will live, [26]and everyone who lives and believes in me will never die. Do you believe this?' [27]She said to him, 'Yes, Lord, I believe that you are the Messiah, the Son of God, the one coming into the world.'

First of all, it was necessary for Lazarus to die. He had to be born again, to be delivered from death into new life, a life that would continue forever, on one side of the grave or the other.

Second, Lazarus was the perfect choice for this experience of the most dramatic of Jesus' miracles. In his commentary on John's Gospel, Jean Vanier (of whom, more later) suggests that the reason Lazarus, as an unmarried man, was living with his two unmarried sisters was that he had some kind of disability, or learning difficulty. It is noticeable that at no point does Lazarus speak, whereas his sisters both seem extremely competent. Vanier does not claim any great insight on this but leaves it as a suggestion, and from my own experience I can see what sense it makes. Most families that I know where someone has a learning difficulty or disability find in that person a treasure, and Mary and Martha's profound grief and their turning to Jesus indicates the depth of their relationship with Lazarus. Even if Lazarus did not have a disability, but was simply ill, he still represents someone who, in the world's eyes, is of little to no value. He does not seem to be a contributing member of society in any measurable economic sense. But, whatever the reason for Lazarus living as an unmarried man in the care of two of his sisters, Jesus sees in him something extraordinarily special, his humanity, his being made in the image of God. In Lazarus, Jesus sees someone for whom it is worth risking his own life.

JOHN 11:28-44

When she had said this, she went back and called her sister Mary, and told her privately, 'The Teacher is here and is calling for you.' [29] And when she heard it, she got up quickly and went to him. [30] Now Jesus had not yet come to the village, but was still at the place where Martha had met him. ³¹ The Jews who were with her in the house, consoling her, saw Mary get up quickly and go out. They followed her because they thought that she was going to the tomb to weep there. ³²When Mary came where Jesus was and saw him, she knelt at his feet and said to him, 'Lord, if you had been here, my brother would not have died.' ³³When Jesus saw her weeping, and the Jews who came with her also weeping, he was greatly disturbed in spirit and deeply moved. ³⁴He said, 'Where have you laid him?' They said to him, 'Lord, come and see.' ³⁵Jesus began to weep. ³⁶So the Jews said, 'See how he loved him!' ³⁷But some of them said, 'Could not he who opened the eyes of the blind man have kept this man from dying?'

³⁸ Then Jesus, again greatly disturbed, came to the tomb. It was a cave, and a stone was lying against it. ³⁹Jesus said, 'Take away the stone.' Martha, the sister of the dead man, said to him, 'Lord, already there is a stench because he has been dead four days.' ⁴⁰Jesus said to her, 'Did I not tell you that if you believed, you would see the glory of God?' ⁴¹So they took away the stone. And Jesus looked upward and said, 'Father, I thank you for having heard me. ⁴²I knew that you always hear me, but I have said this for the sake of the crowd standing here, so that they may believe that you sent me.' ⁴³When he had said this, he cried with a loud voice, 'Lazarus, come out!' ⁴⁴The dead man came out, his hands and feet bound with strips of cloth, and his face wrapped in a cloth. Jesus said to them, 'Unbind him, and let him go.'

Jesus engages with Mary and Martha in different ways. He challenges their faith, calling them to look at him and see the reality that he offers, not to be deceived by the falsity of the power of death. By raising their brother from the dead, he offers them a new way to see the world. He heals their eyes.

Mary and Martha, with newly corrected vision, respond by further deepening their commitment to being disciples of Jesus.

How can we see like Mary and Martha? Jesus' answer is to point to himself. We need to first see Jesus, and then to see what he does. But our eyes need to be opened to that by a response in faith: we must not say we believe when we don't, but we trust what he says and sees, beyond that which we think we see. His sight is better than ours.

In his presence, the lies of death cannot be maintained. What we see we value, and Jesus sees the reality of the life of Lazarus, the purpose of his suffering and the conclusion of his story. The result is the most dramatic of changes, the overcoming of death.

The overcoming of the death of Lazarus shows the extravagant generosity of God. The raising of Lazarus is Jesus' invitation to the world to see life as more real, more fundamental than death. In the end, Mary and Martha's vision is corrected. They see not only Lazarus but the abundance of life in Christ. The authorities, however, resist Jesus' invitation. They see through eyes of the old, evil age, in which resurrected life is a threat rather than a gift.

What might it look like for God to correct your vision?
To where, whom, or what might God be calling your attention?
What might God want you to see that you've never truly seen before?

The beginning of dethroning Mammon is to see clearly so that we may value properly. What we see may be small, and its true value only perceived through the eyes of faith.

One of my heroes, a man called Cardinal Văn Thuận, was held prisoner for many years in Vietnam after the fall of South Vietnam to the Communist regime of Hanoi in 1974. There are many wonderful stories from him about the grace of God, but let me put two side by side to illustrate God's generosity.

While he was in prison, every day, he managed to celebrate mass, putting himself in communion with Christians around the world and with the living presence of Christ. Though he had no books, he celebrated using the liturgy that he had memorised over the years. Typically he took one grain of rice and a few drops of rice wine, offering them up in the palm of his hand.

The generosity of God kept him deeply embedded in the Church, faithful to Jesus Christ, through long years of solitary confinement and torture. He was not taken out of the situation, which for most of us would be beyond our imagination, but found himself embraced every day by the generosity of God in a grain of rice and a mere taste of rice wine, unfolding the whole presence of the creator of the universe.

After he was released, Văn Thuận went back to Italy, where he rose to become a Cardinal and one of the closest collaborators of Pope John Paul II. In the year 2000, he was asked to give the Lent talks to the Curia (the senior clergy around the Pope) at the Vatican, which were published in a wonderful book called *Testimony of Hope*. He starts off by saying that what he loves most about God are God's faults. Among them is 'ludicrous over-generosity'. We see that generosity in the beautiful story of the marriage at Cana (John 2:1-12), when, after fears that the feast will be a disaster and the honour of the hosts undermined, enough wine is made for an entire village to drink itself under the table. There was far more than would ever be needed at any normal wedding feast! It is a picture of the creative abundance of God, and points to the nature of Jesus as God himself. When he makes something, he makes so much of it that it must overflow from us to meet the needs of the world around us. I find this one of the most miraculous and wonderful images of the God whom we serve.

Where else in the Bible — or indeed in your own life — has God responded to a need or request with over-generosity?

But what has any of this got to do with money?

It seems to me that money is so powerful in the way we experience it that it carries almost the same weight as death. Not quite, of course, because in the end death overcomes money. As they say, 'You can't take it with you' or 'A shroud has no pockets'.

Despite the reality that money is only for now, its power over our thinking and imagination is extraordinary. Money makes a big noise about itself and calls us to value it, over and above anything else in our lives. It captures our attention in small and large ways.

I am a fan of detective stories, and for many years, especially when a bit weary, have turned to Dorothy L. Sayers. One of her last stories was called *Busman's Honeymoon*. There is one scene in it where the very wealthy detective hero, Lord Peter

Wimsey, is talking to a vicar of the local parish (the story is set in the 1920s or early 1930s). He gets out his wallet and produces a £5 note as a contribution to some cause of the vicar's. As he produces the note, everyone's eyes are fixed on it and the vicar comments that it has been a long time since he saw a real treasury note. The money attracts all eyes and its casual flourishing by Lord Peter tells everyone in the scene that he is a person of immense wealth as well as rank.

As early as the first century, in his Epistle, James writes: 'Has not God chosen the poor in the world to be rich in faith and to be heirs of the kingdom that he has promised to those who love him? But you have dishonoured the poor. Is it not the rich who oppress you? Is it not they who drag you into court?' (James 2:5-6). Money warps our judgement of wealth and corrupts our appreciation of individuals. The appearance of a very rich man or woman at any event causes a fluttering, and a clustering of those who seek a little of the magic to rub off on them. It has always been so.

The reason for the flutter and attraction is that money clearly buys advantage. It even buys life. The difference in life expectancy at birth between the richest and poorest parts of the UK is as much as ten years. The areas may be geographically very close; from Everton in Liverpool to Formby on the coast further north is no more than fifteen miles, but you gain an average of nine months of life expectancy at birth with each mile you travel.

Wealth buys visible privacy, large rooms, high walls and big gardens. It buys leisure, opportunities to spend time as one chooses and other people to do the chores. It buys company, friends, opportunity and education. But it does not buy God.

On the one hand, we have the overflowing generosity of God, which reaches out in abundant provision to the solitary prisoner, even to the dead. On the other hand, we have the siren call of money which tells us that it alone is effective in changing our lives and our world and meeting our every need.

Given the lies that money presents us with – the way it stands before us and says, 'Look at me, you see value when you see me' – what opens our eyes to the abundant and excessively generous God? The contest between God and Mammon – the need to dethrone the latter – is not a matter simply of competing estimates of value. It is a question of truth and lies. Mammon lies by distorting our vision, while God brings truth and perception into our lives. Seeing correctly enables us to value correctly, to distinguish between truth and lies.

The Bible continually speaks to us. Throughout Scripture the Spirit of God opens people's eyes to the reality of the world around them; and it does the same for us as we read it. The story of Lazarus is one full of observers and participants in these extraordinary events.

There are onlookers, the crowd, who show themselves cynical and questioning, asking why Jesus could not have healed Lazarus before he died. There are Martha and Mary, despairing and bereft, questioning, yet with a deep sense that, in ways they do not understand, Jesus is the answer. The disciples trail along behind, increasingly confused. There is Lazarus, and finally Jesus, the only one seeing correctly.

They all see the same thing, yet they perceive differently. All except Jesus perceive power in death. The response may be different but the acceptance of the value of death, its definitive power, is common to all except Jesus. Those who love us and are close to us are horrified both by death, and by its impact, its smell. In Lent, to some extent, we remember that we are all Lazarus, all suffering from the death of sin, the turning inwards, the growing darkness, the inextricable weakness that leads us towards death. None of us can escape that, whether it comes sooner or later. Our bodies are finite.

But when we meet Jesus something extraordinary happens. Most often it is not that we seek him out, but suddenly this figure comes to us, even when we are entirely dead and lost, and calls to us, 'Lazarus, come out!'

In recent weeks, I have been reading the Bible with a group of people who are interested in the Christian faith. The discussions have been demanding, in a wonderful way. But what has been most exciting for me is their response to the overwhelming and abundant generosity of God, the God who breaks in with 'more God' than anyone can consume locally. For Lazarus, that must have been part of the experience of his resurrection. God breaks in with such force that death is compelled to flee and Lazarus comes forth. He is the same Lazarus: they recognise him, and he goes back to his family. But the excessive life of God has poured in and driven out death.

Lazarus almost immediately becomes a living testimony to Jesus. That, of course, has its own problems because as a witness to Jesus, he becomes a threat to those who oppose Jesus. They start planning to kill him as well as Jesus.

I often wonder why Jesus picks Lazarus to bring back from the dead. Death would have been an everyday event around him, and it continued even in his presence. He is

not a magic-worker. Jesus did not go around Galilee right-
ing each and every wrong that he came across. He was not a
Harry Potter figure. The reality was very different. For most
people who met Jesus, life went on. They might remember an
extraordinary event, such as 5,000 people being fed miracu-
lously with food to spare, or a blind man seeing, but they did
not *perceive* differently as a result. The preoccupations of daily
life and need prevented them from changing their vision.

That is the point for me. I first had a clear sense of the
breaking in of Jesus to my life in October 1975. My life went
on as it had before. There were the same problems, and there
were joys. There were people I got on with and people I found
difficult. But there was a new and abundant presence in my
life that was completely and totally transformative so that I
was no longer the person I had been. From that moment, the
world was a different place because it was suffused with
the presence of Christ. I had to learn, and continue to learn,
to perceive differently as a result.

So, in a sense, each of us is Lazarus, and for each of us
Jesus' abundant life is there to overcome all that is deathly,
unpleasant and decaying about us, and to lead us into a place
of grace and generosity. He sees all of us and everything about
us, the seen and the unseen.

But, in this abundance, there is also a challenge to the
self-centredness of our economy, and of Mammon. Mammon
is absolutely finite and quite indivisible, even if mechanisms
are created that give the illusion of an endless supply of money
and finance. If we spend money on one thing, we can't spend
it on another. If we spend enough of it, it runs out (for some
of us, 'enough' is not a lot). Worst of all, despite the fact that

there is not a lot of it compared to the abundance of God, and it is finite compared to the infinity of God, it claims to define the value of everyone we meet and to define our lives. By contrast, God offers freedom, growth and choice.

This is where God's ridiculous economics are ridiculous by secular standards, yet they dethrone Mammon and demonstrate that they are far wiser than the best economic theories of the world.

The giving up of his own life, the pouring out of his life for others – for you and me so that we may know God – does not expend his life, yet brings an infinite amount of life to us. The laws of economics say that spending in one area gives revenue in another, and they all balance out. Jesus' economics are so much bigger than this. They do not balance. The spending of God's life gives an infinite quantity of life to the world.

Put infinity of love and possibility into the finite and limited system that is the global economy and the strain dethrones Mammon. All of a sudden there is a force in the way the world works that has the possibility of changing almost everything we do: there is a corrective to the way that the whole of humanity experiences need and necessity, adequacy and abundance. 'Ridiculous', or divine, economics rises to show us that what we see *is* what we value, and thus there is a need to change what we see.

This is how we respond to the economics of God. We are ourselves to be those who are generous, who trust that when we give away, more will come back. Let me go back to Jean Vanier. In 1964, he started a community with himself and two people with severe learning difficulties. That single small community has now grown into a huge number of people, in many communities around the world. Jean gave all that he had, and in human economics one person's all is very little. In God's 'ridiculous', divine economics, that gift has transformed attitudes to disability and to learning difficulties, and taught people that the apparently powerful may be blessed by the weak if they allow themselves to be, and may find themselves incapable of blessing the weak when they stand stuck in their own power.

At the heart of this economics is doing things not for people or to people, but *with* people. Vanier and those in his communities live with each other, and in standing alongside each other create a whole which is greater than the sum of its parts.

The more difficult part of what we see is not from our individual perspectives but at the 'big-picture' level. It is a normal part of the prophetic ministry of the Church to challenge the way our societies see the world, and thus to challenge what they value. When this happens, people often complain that church leaders, whether bishops or others, are interfering in politics.

Imagine a ship sailing up the English Channel, coming in from the Atlantic. As it approaches the Scilly Isles, the lighthouse signals the danger of rocks which in past generations have claimed so many lives. In 1707 more than a thousand men were lost from the fleet of the Royal Navy when, not knowing their latitude because of the absence of reliable chronometers, they struck rocks close to the Scilly Isles. The crew were confused and blind to the danger. Had even one passenger known the danger, it would not have been 'interfering' to have made a fuss. Everything needed to be seen differently.

It is the same for the economy today. We are simply looking at it in the wrong way. We give Mammon authority as though it were divine when it is a fraudulent misrepresentation of inevitability. Reality, history, ultimate value and eternal hope are found not in the economy but in God himself, who has acted once and for all decisively in Jesus Christ. Christ who overcame death is not subordinate to the economy.

There is a great danger of this view being seen as Utopian, theocratic or merely naive. I am not pretending that the rules of normal economics do not apply, or that there is a Christian way of ignoring them. Supply and demand, risk and reward, the gift of the free market to locate goods well, the need for balance in the flows of money within the economy, all continue to be relevant. But they are not God. They guide us but must not be allowed to control us. Let us take two examples, first of inequality, and second of indebtedness and the creation of credit through the workings of the financial system.

Inequality has grown more and more sharply in the Western world, in almost every society, and particularly over the past thirty years. In the richest countries in our world, including the UK, the richest 10 per cent of the population now on average earn almost ten times the income of the poorest 10 per cent.[1] The dangers of inequality are often obscured with ideas like the trickle-down theory, which claims that the extreme wealth of the few will 'trickle down' through their investments and spending and that all members of the population will benefit. The theory is summed up by the cliché 'a rising tide lifts all boats'.

But is this really true? There is limited evidence to support the theory, not least because trickle-down does not account for human nature. As will be seen in a later chapter, rather than money 'trickling down', we tend to hold on to what we have. Since John Maynard Keynes, it has been recognised that, rather than spending, the very wealthy choose to save more (what Keynes called 'hoarding') and preserve their wealth. Inequality is in fact deeply destabilising of a society, and yet our economic and fiscal system increases it ever further.

We need to challenge this aspect of the rule of Mammon, to take seriously that God is on the side of the poor – even the ultimate poor, like Lazarus, who are considered to have no economic value. To be on their side, to be with them as Jesus was with them, and as Jean Vanier is with his community, does not mean paternalistically sharing their sufferings, but challenging the reason for them. Part of our role in dethroning Mammon is to be part of the call for his societal dethroning, as seen in the actions of governments and organisations – which may be fostering inequality – and not just in our own wallets.

Consider the groups, communities and institutions of which you are a member. How do they see the world?
In what way has their vision been affected by Mammon?
How might you challenge that?

Second, recent reflection on the causes and nature of the crash of 2008 have pointed not at individual banks as the principal cause of the trouble, but at the way the banking system works. The former chairman of one of the UK's main

financial regulators, Lord Adair Turner, presents a particularly compelling argument to this effect in his recent book,
Between Debt and the Devil.

He argues that from the early 1990s the ability of our banks
to create money electronically meant that while the economy
was growing at anything up to 3 per cent each year, the level
of debt in the UK economy as a whole was growing at about
5 per cent each year. Similar figures apply all over the world,
including China since 2008. So the total amount of debt was
growing faster than the economy, until there was too much
and it became unstable.

To make matters worse, over 70 per cent of all the new
debt was not going into things that made the economy more
efficient or that would produce a high rate of return in the
future to pay off the debt. Mainly it went into mortgages,
often sold to the poorer end of society, the so-called 'junk
loans'. The 2010 book, *The Big Short,* recently made into a
blockbuster film, dramatised powerfully the fact that many
bankers were not only aware this was a bad idea, but were
also contemptuous of their clients, both the people who
borrowed and the people who lent.

To put it simply, we found ourselves with a banking
system that was both out of control and uncontrollable. It is
a system that generates debt for people who can't pay it back,
owed to those who can't afford to lend it in the first place.

And we wonder why people were surprised that it ended
in tears.

This is really not the place for a discussion of fractional
reserve banking (the idea that banks can lend out money that
they do not actually have), but it does provoke some very

serious questions about the way the markets saw the world, and the resulting way that societies, central bankers, customers, you name it, saw and see the world.

Once again, what is seen is valued. Markets are very persuasive influences: they claim sovereignty over perception. Thus the 'right' price of something traded in the market is what the market says, even if that price bears no reasonable relation to the value of the effort put in, the imagination involved, or the underlying costs and lives of the producers.

The value put on such things by God is very different. In God's eyes, the infinite value of the human is the same for every single one of us, regardless of our role in the economy – whether we are a producer, a trader, a consumer, or none of these things. God's perception of value is not that of the market. And the market is not as rational or informed as it appears. Rather, it is the emotional conclusion of a particular view of supply and demand over a specific period. Often the result is fair – in a complex society, the market is without doubt an extremely efficient mechanism of distribution. But it can also cause human suffering on an unacceptable, but often invisible, scale.

Markets are visible. The price of something is in front of us, in hard numbers on a screen. People are very often invisible, hidden behind collective terms such as 'farmers' or 'producers'.

This confrontation of values is often turned into right-wing and left-wing terms, but it is far deeper than that. Essentially it is about how we see. There is thus not just a personal or a community dimension, but also a societal dimension to this story. The poor, the unseen and the uncounted are Lazarus.

The poor represent 'the ones that Jesus loves' today. There are parallels to the questions we ask about poverty that run right through the story.

First of all, Jesus delays going to Lazarus. We often ask ourselves why there is poverty, why God does not just step in and do something about it? Part of the answer is in the freedom that God gives us *not* to embrace divine generosity. Jesus weeps by the tomb of Lazarus, and the onlookers wonder why, if he cared for Lazarus so much, he could not stop him dying? The question can be put to us in terms of global poverty. We too weep at poverty, but then we need to recognise that it is in our hands to change the world in which we live.

Many of us will recognise the statement by the Brazilian Archbishop Hélder Câmara, who said, 'When I feed the poor they call me a saint; when I ask why they are poor, they call me a communist.'

In living out the economy of God, we are called to do both, because we do not see only what is before us – the reality of death, the inevitability of poverty – but we see the life and abundance of Jesus. We need a switch in our seeing that means we see as God sees. If what we see, we value, then how transformational is it to see through the eyes of Christ?

So the next step in applying this passage to our own discipleship is to pray, and to pray that we may begin to have the eyes of Jesus for the world around us. Then we may begin to see the reality that God has created and intends for our flourishing.

I have to say that I do not write this with any great sense of comfort. To see the world as God sees it is to see huge beauty

in every person, and the infinite provision of God that can
come through us. But it is also to see a life in which my autonomy, my control over what I want and what I do, my desire
to ration my love rather than to let it flow out abundantly
(because deep down I always fear it might run out) has to be
surrendered to the God of abundance and grace.

Mary and Martha both struggle with this. When Jesus says
to them, 'Your brother will rise again' (John 11:23), they
reply that they know there will be a resurrection (of course,
they imply a condition to what they say, which is that there
is a resurrection but 'that's a rather long time away and you
could have avoided this death').

Jesus tells them that they must change their view. It is
not an easy thing, because it puts them in the place of risk.
Opening a tomb exposed people to the risk of infection, and
to the stench of death. Translated into our age, it requires us
to be committed to being with those whose dying makes a
stink, but that in turn will cause us to stink. Jesus' enemies
called that being sinners. We commit to being with them in
Jesus' way – to seeing as God sees – and then we find that life
breaks in through Jesus.

The trouble is that everything around us tells us something different. In a book I was reading recently, the writer
remarked that at the local community level, people find faith
quite possible. They go to church and find people who are
often welcoming and friendly. They find they are loved and
valued within the church community. But when they look
into the world of the everyday, in the supermarket, going
to and from work, in the place where they live, or simply
walking down the street, they see thousands upon thousands

of people who appear to be going along perfectly happily without God. It is at this point that the description in many marketing surveys of religion as a leisure activity (by implication, something we can take or leave) seems to make much more sense. What we see we value, and when we see a world in which people live happily without God, that world seems safe and comfortable, and therefore often more valued than the alternative. By contrast, living life with Jesus seems like an uncomfortable and costly risk.

What aspects of your daily life can make your faith feel
uncomfortable and risky?
How could seeing things through God's eyes help you?

To see things with God's eyes is not to see them as dour and terrible, nor to view all those we meet in the street who appear to be getting along quite happily without him as bad people. We are not called to be judgemental, looking down on people and feeling that we have some special secret.

Our response is to be quite the reverse. We are to see Jesus in the midst of the people that we meet, and, being with him, to grow in confidence in the knowledge that what he brings in his abundance and grace brings also human flourishing and life in a new way.

It all sounds a bit mystical – to suggest that we are to see Jesus in those around us, when normally all we see is people getting in our way when we are trying to get into the shortest queue at the checkouts. It is actually much simpler than that. We see Jesus around us when we start the day by praying that we will do so. Because of his abundance and grace, we are almost always surprised.

Can you remember a time when God met you in a surprising or unexpected way?
In who or what did God reveal himself to you?
Did that experience in any way change the way you see the world?

What we see we value. Let us see the presence of Jesus, and recognise that God's (ridiculous) divine economics overwhelms the economics that Mammon offers us with its implication that that is all there is to be seen in this world. When we see with God's eyes, we discover that there is far, far more on offer.

What we measure controls us

Key text *Luke 19*
Zacchaeus the Tax Collector

In the previous chapter, I started with the problem that what we see, we value. In this chapter, I'd like to expand on that by paying particular attention to how what we consider to be valuable is tied to those things we can measure – specifically, those things we can measure in financial terms. 'What we can measure, we control' is very much an assumed (if unspoken) dogma of our secular age. The reality is that what we measure (at least economically) tends to control us, or at least define us. At a national level, premium value is placed on measurables, like Gross Domestic Product (GDP), the state of the economy, the rates of investment by companies, and the financial prospects for the future. Notoriously, if it's not measured it tends not to be managed. People may keep a tight control on measurable aspects of their lives, such as the household budgets, salary, even use of time. Yet the same people may be entirely unaware of the state of their relationships, the condition of their marriage, the happiness of their children. The degree to which Mammon is enthroned in each of our lives, or the culture of our society, is uncomfortably revealed by the degree to which we often disproportionally value the things we can readily measure.

One of the biggest gaps in the ways that the wealth of our country is measured is that it ignores what is voluntary and unpaid. A bizarre illustration of the relationship between the way one looks at value and the impact of money is that if someone moves from a paid job to doing the same job on a voluntary basis, the measured economy shrinks – albeit to a very small extent.

Let me give an example. When I was a parish priest, I was working in a parish that had some financial difficulties and relatively few churchgoers. In consequence, almost everything was done by volunteers. Someone came in to help with the administration in the parish office. Other volunteers ran our children and youth work. The music was also handled voluntarily.

However, as the number of people coming to church grew and the church became more involved in the life of the community, the demands on the volunteers became excessive. In order to be able to focus more effectively on what we were trying to do as a church, we took on some paid staff. The first person to be taken on was a parish administrator. She had been helping us voluntarily insofar as she could, given that she needed to earn her own living, but she now became an employee. The fact that she had more time to work in the church was very useful, and made a big difference. But the fact that she was employed did not change her capacity or her qualities. She was still the same welcoming, effective and efficient person she had been as a volunteer. Yet from the point of view of the Gross Domestic Product of the United Kingdom, by taking her on as a paid employee, even, at first, for similar hours to those she had been doing voluntarily, we increased the national wealth. We had, in theory, created a job. Of course, in practice, we had not created any jobs at all. The same amount of time was being spent on the work as previously, except it was now being paid for. The same applied when, with other churches, we took on a youth worker to support the work we were doing with young people in the community. It was effective to do that, but it did not mean that we had suddenly caused something to happen that was not happening before; we were merely doing it more formally and more professionally.

If you add up the monetary value of all the voluntary work done under their umbrella, churches and other faith groups in the United Kingdom are estimated to contribute over £3.3 billion to the economy every year. Other estimates suggest that members of the Church of England alone give 22.3 million hours each month in voluntary service. This includes everything from helping out at local schools, to running food banks, to opening churches to be used as homeless shelters and caring for the elderly. In the wider world, we see a similar situation in the work done by carers for members of their family. This work is not usually remunerated but saves the national economy tens of billions of pounds every year. Yet it is not measured, and thus is often undervalued or ignored.

The consequences of ignoring the voluntary, or the non-remunerated, are widespread and disastrous.

It demeans those who act from love, rather than out of hope for gain. The two are not, of course, contradictory. Plenty of people serve with love in areas for which they are paid well. The so-called 'caring professions' are an obvious example. Good teachers love their pupils. Good surgeons exhibit a passionate care for patients. Even in very hard-driven areas one comes across people whose desire to do things right, and to value and respect colleagues, speaks of a motivation including but going far beyond what they are paid. Soldiers follow leaders who care for them. Field Marshal Montgomery often used to stop at a pre-battle briefing and say to some hapless and doubtless petrified soldier, 'What is your most valuable possession?' 'My rifle, sir?' 'Nonsense, your life; and I aim to ensure you keep it.'

Yet the attention paid to what is measured, which in modern society often means what is measured numerically, can lead to a demeaning of people who do things without economic reward. Mammon brushes past them, spurning them as unimportant, little people.

What are the other measurables (apart from money) that control your life? Try to list them. In what way do they influence your habits and motivations?
What can you not imagine life without? Make a list.
How many of those things are measurable and how many are immeasurable?

The parent or family member who stays at home or refuses a promotion to be with a child with disabilities is not considered to contribute. Yet the sacrifice and care they demonstrate is extraordinary. A spouse who supports their partner at the cost of their own career is seen as second-rate, or lacking ambition.

Within the life of the Church, we often see a similar attitude. The contemplative religious life – a commitment to live in a community of prayer and mutual love and sharing, either for a defined term or for life – is a model that has never been very highly regarded within Protestantism. Yet, until the Reformation, the vast majority of renewals of spiritual life in the Church were associated with these contemplative communities.

There is often a pseudo-humorous denigration of people in the religious life. The Community of St Anselm, involving a quasi-monastic commitment of ten months to a community based at Lambeth Palace, has had a transforming effect on the life of many others who work there. The presence of a group of people for whom Christ is the fascination, and prayer the biggest part of daily life, changes the DNA of the place. It is anything but funny.

'But what do they do?' I am often asked. Is there anything practical? No, there is not, unless, of course, you consider prayer to be practical, which it most emphatically is. Even within the Church, something that does not produce measurable results is seen as doubtful. I will talk more about this in Chapter 3.

One of the great distractions of clergy involves buildings. Often this work has to be done, and done very well. The Church of England has roughly 16,000 buildings, of which 12,500 are listed, noted as of historic interest. They need work. As I discovered as a parish priest, old buildings are often unfriendly to those attending church, inflexible for community use and staggeringly cold. So they need updating, as has been done in every generation since church building started.

Yet there is, I discovered, a perverse temptation in building things. It can sometimes be done, as T. S. Eliot puts it in

Murder in the Cathedral, by succumbing to the fourth temptation, 'to do the right thing for the wrong reason'. In a wonderful book by Rumer Godden, *In This House of Brede*, an elderly abbess falls for what is called 'stone fever', a desire to mark her tenure in stone and buildings.

To point to something solid is deeply and satisfyingly positive. Those who built Liverpool Cathedral started it in 1904 and finished in 1978. They were wonderful craftsmen who, when they retired, could point to it from almost anywhere in the City of Liverpool, and say proudly, 'I built that.' They were right to do so.

Parish priests who have worked steadily and well, leading people to faith, serving the poor, loving everyone in the parish, contributing to the life of the local church and the community, may also spend their lives in that craft, and a great and wonderful craft it is. There may not be any tangible change to see, although many lives will have been improved and valued. It is a temptation to say they have done nothing, because unlike the reassuring tangibility of buildings, we cannot easily see or measure what they have done.

But what is not measurable may be valuable beyond measure. Not allowing it to define us in the way that the tangible does in some way demeans us, or demeans those who do intangible things. Implicitly, we say they are lesser. Money shouts very loudly: 'Look at me, look at me, see what I am doing and see how special I am.' Mammon draws our gaze away from things that are more worthy of our attention, but have not been given the badge of a comparable monetary value.

Looking at your life, what gives you most joy and happiness?
Of the things you value, which are tangible
and which more intangible?
How balanced is the spread of your attention between them?

I am reminded of a story I heard from a community in Nairobi. A local pastor, Pastor Luke Jakoywa, wanted to begin a school but did not have the teachers he needed, nor the money to pay them with. One day, he approached a few young people in the neighbourhood who were looking for employment, asking them if they were willing to help. He asked them, since they were spending the day doing nothing for nothing, would they be willing to do something (useful) for nothing? There was still no money to pay them but they would add enormous value to the local community, and use their gifts and talents to help others.

This is how Pastor Luke recruited teachers for his school. He showed the young people how to see value, to approach value and to 'value' it, in service to others. Seven years on, the school and community centre, called Sheepcare, has more than five hundred children in both primary and secondary education. The teachers draw a meagre salary, just enough to keep going, but the value of what they do – and the value of the skills they have – goes far beyond any financial value that can be applied to it.

The problem with materialism – this prioritising of the tangible – is not that it exists, but that it dominates. It shouts so loudly that it overrides our caring about other things of greater value.

A second example of not valuing things that are not easily measured is the example of the environment. In much of the world, people are experiencing 'increasingly strong and more frequent extreme weather events; change in seasonal weather patterns; rising levels of sea water; acidification of sea water and depleted fishing grounds; the devastating effects of pollution; deforestation, and destructive mining and energy extraction and transportation practices'.[1]

In the UK, we have not yet felt the worst effects of climate change in our world. Floods come more frequently and more devastatingly, as in the northwest of England in 2016, but they are dismissed as 'weather'. We will not see, beyond doubt, which bits of 'weather' were in fact climate change until many years have passed, and then it will be too late. The consequences of climate change do not as yet significantly affect the national economy. They are not currently measurable as climate change, and therefore their value – or, in this case, great cost – remains invisible.

Within the environmental movement, another aspect of impact that is not adequately measured is the flourishing of future generations. The effect of much of our individual and collective impact on the environment will not be something we see in our own lifetimes. People talk about significant sea level rises by 2100 – some generations away.

Notoriously, in the calculations of economics and business, costs in the far future have no present value. This is the effect of what is known technically as discounting. Clearly, something I am going to have to pay in ten years has a different impact on me from something I am going to have to pay in ten minutes. Something that my great-grandchildren will have to pay in 100 years has even less impact on my present financial situation. Businesses and pension funds try to estimate the future impact of what they will have to pay by turning future liabilities into present costs by calculating their value in today's money. But we all know that there is an element of illusion in this. Costs projected 100 years ahead are extraordinarily uncertain. We need to put a number on them to do the calculation, but it will only be educated guesswork. The correct answer is probably 'lots and lots'.

The result is that intergenerational impacts are ignored.

Yet intergenerational ethics is a key element of reflecting the nature of God, who sees all time and space in one glance. Mammon rises up and tells us that this is so far in the future that it is neither to be measured nor a cause for concern; more than that, we surely owe more to today's generation. Yet God says, 'All time is mine', and the Old Testament is full of the consciousness of responsibility for subsequent generations. God's covenant with David (2 Samuel 7) is a covenant for all time. David's own sense of blessing concerns not just the present, but also the future, because of what his descendants are promised.

In what way does your care for future generations impinge on your daily life?
What habits or practices might you change if you were to value intergenerational ethics more highly?

God's repeated promise to Abraham is that his descendants will be as numerous as the stars of the sky (Genesis 15:5,

22:17, 26:4). For these great figures of the Old Testament, their own sense of value was tied up in their descendants, in what would happen in distant future times. One of the most destructive elements of the despotic rule of Mammon is that our sense of being part of the flow of the generations is eliminated, and increasingly we live for now (or 'for the present moment'), with the sense that we will not be around to worry about the future. 'Eat and drink, for tomorrow we die' is the catchphrase of the Hedonists, quoted by Paul in 1 Corinthians 15:32.

The other aspect of our enthroning of Mammon that I want to consider is the sheer power it has to lead us down the wrong track concerning what enables human beings to flourish.

The period 1992–2008 was one of the longest of uninterrupted economic growth that this country has known (at least as measured by Gross Domestic Product – there you go, now I'm doing it). As I have already mentioned, in this period the principal and, at times, only way in which the economy continued to grow was through increasing levels of personal indebtedness. That applied not only within the UK (although we were among the worst) but even more so in the USA. At the same time, even in Europe where personal loans had historically been relatively low, they rose dramatically, and savings diminished.

In other words, what economists call the consumer sector, or the personal sector, or household sector, ran a deficit. Collectively, year by year, we borrowed more and more. It is an old truism of economics that the sums of money in the economy must balance. If one group of people is running a deficit then someone else must be running a surplus. In the UK, over the period in question, government also ran something of a deficit (although not an enormous one), and companies in general, taken as a whole, ran a huge surplus. In other words, they cut back on investment, for which they would need to borrow, and stored up value. This was paid out either in the form of dividends, through share buy-backs, or as higher salaries for senior managers. Rates of inequality grew, as those who had access to money managed to increase their income significantly, while those at the bottom of the pile simply increased their debt.

The result, as we all know, was the catastrophe of 2008 and the Great Recession that followed. All the chickens came home to roost. The country found itself struggling with consumers who could not borrow any more. Individuals started repaying debt. For years, the government had taxed banks and other financial institutions on profits they had made by lending too much. In other words, the money had never really been there. It was measured, and that measurement controlled the way we counted, but the measurement was an illusion. As a result the national accounts got completely out of control. Once everyone realised this, and experienced an economy that was no longer growing, it shrank even more significantly.

To this day, we are cutting social benefits, reducing investment in infrastructure, and struggling to make ends meet. Research commissioned in 2016 by the Centre for Regional Economic and Social Research noted that 'as a general rule, the more deprived the local authority the greater the financial loss'.[2] That is, those who are poorest – and seen, by the way we measure things, to be the least valuable – are those who have borne the brunt of spending cuts.

The steady drip-feed of increasing consumer spending was the motor for the economy. Mammon told us that the answer to poverty was to spend more. Mammon lied.

The silver lining to these dark clouds was that it appeared for a while that Mammon had been dethroned. There was a loss of faith in finance as the solution to all human ills, or in economic growth as the way to the perfect society. By 2011, debt in the household sector had fallen, and salaries among the highest-paid were also beginning to be restrained. Even those who worked in the City of London's financial sector acknowledged that warnings of the dangers of unhindered greed, which had driven much of the expansion in finance, had been ignored.

The disasters associated with the crash were linked to the fact that the measured economy had looked quite healthy. The shouts of jubilation that the economy was expanding had drowned out all other concerns, in particular, those things which are immeasurable. We were not valuing the things that we were not measuring. Some groups had spoken out, church leaders in many countries, some economists, even some politicians. The problem is that Mammon is not merely very loud and persuasive but also very powerful and attractive. It all comes back to how and what we measure.

Try arguing that a measured increase in national wealth is less important than paying back debt, or incurring less debt in the first place. Try arguing that less is better. It is part of being human to want to own, to possess, to enjoy an illusion of being independent, of not relying on others. Saint Benedict in his sixth-century Rule[3] for monasteries dealt with the same problem. He emphasises that private property in the monastery is wrong, forbidden, completely impossible. Even so, he has to set out penalties for breaking this rule. Human nature resists dethroning Mammon.

As a result, even after the catastrophe of 2008 and the ensuing Great Recession, something extraordinary is already happening. Once again, consumer debt is rising quite sharply. People are talking about the end of the 'years of austerity', by which they do not mean that on a sensible basis it is possible for people to spend a great deal more, but that with very low interest rates it is possible to borrow a great deal more and spend it on things we want.

An example of this is 'Black Friday', a recent American import, which drives up consumer spending ever further in the run-up to Christmas. It drowns out any voice that suggests there should be celebration without huge excess – something that I will challenge a little later in this book.

I am beginning to sound like Scrooge, and may in fact in a moment write 'Bah! Humbug!' The celebrations of Christmas are wonderful, and throughout human history, the middle of the winter has been seen in the northern hemisphere as a good time to rejoice in the hope that summer will return, with its long days, warm weather and abundant harvest. It has always been a time of getting together, of parties and the enjoyment of human relationship.

The best advertisements around Christmas (and there are quite a lot of good ones) suggest this in one way or another. The products they propose are set in the context of families getting together, of friends being welcomed. These are excellent things. And yet so much of the advertising is also about a simple call to buy more. Struggling with a malfunctioning app which enables me to have the Bible on my tablet, I looked up the website for its owner. Unsurprisingly, it was run by Christians. Yet the first thing that hit me when I opened their website was a banner saying 'huge discounts for Black Friday'.

The problem is not the discounts, or even the materialism. It is that the voice of money and Mammon is so much louder than the things we don't measure – including the things of ultimate value, such as the word of God.

---

*What examples come to mind for you of situations where
the shout of Mammon drowns out or masks
the things that really matter?*

In Luke's Gospel, chapters 18–19 take us to the very beginning of Holy Week. They cover the last few miles of Jesus' journey to Jerusalem, his triumphal entry into the city, and the cleansing of the Temple. This section goes to the heart of what we are looking at in this chapter – about what we value, about what matters. It has a lot in it about money, and about dethroning Mammon. It also has a lot in it about learning to see well so that, in valuing what we see, we may value well. The answer to the power of money is seen in a right attitude to people, to worship and to God. The right attitude to people is seen by the way in which Jesus deals with the often highly conflictual encounters that he has in this chapter.

Luke's Palm Sunday narrative consists of a series of dramatic encounters between Jesus and different manifestations of

Mammon. In each individual episode, there is a clash of values. In each episode, Jesus invites us to dethrone Mammon, and to see the world through healed and holy eyes.

LUKE 18:35-43

As he approached Jericho, a blind man was sitting by the roadside begging. [36]When he heard a crowd going by, he asked what was happening. [37]They told him, 'Jesus of Nazareth is passing by.' [38]Then he shouted, 'Jesus, Son of David, have mercy on me!' [39]Those who were in front sternly ordered him to be quiet; but he shouted even more loudly, 'Son of David, have mercy on me!' [40]Jesus stood still and ordered the man to be brought to him; and when he came near, he asked him, [41]'What do you want me to do for you?' He said, 'Lord, let me see again.' [42]Jesus said to him, 'Receive your sight; your faith has saved you.' [43]Immediately he regained his sight and followed him, glorifying God; and all the people, when they saw it, praised God.

On the way to Jerusalem, Jesus and his disciples encounter a blind beggar as they go into Jericho. In Mammon's kingdom, as the disciples attest, this is someone who contributes nothing to the economy. He is in fact an economic drain, and therefore of no value. There is nothing new about the voice of wealth drowning out the realities of human dignity. The clash of values here is not between Jesus and the beggar, but rather, it is between Jesus and 'those who were in front' (v. 39) – that is, his own disciples who ordered the blind man to be quiet.

The disciples do not see any significance or importance at all in a poor, blind man, who begs outside the city.

Jesus overcomes his disciples' failure to see the value of the blind man. The irony of the scene is that the blind man sees Jesus more clearly than the disciples or anyone in the crowd. His spiritual sight overcomes his physical blindness, and is turned into full vision. He ends up seeing fully, and follows Jesus, rejoicing.

The second encounter is with Zacchaeus, the chief tax collector in Jericho. Zacchaeus can see perfectly adequately, but the trouble is he does not want to be seen for who he really is. The crowd ignore him, the second time in the chapter that Jesus' followers turn their backs on someone. Being a small man and unable to get to the front, he is forced to climb a tree, in order to see Jesus. As with the beggar, Jesus notices him, calls him down and enables him to see himself and his future. Zacchaeus sees so well that he invites Jesus to his home, and Jesus sees true value so clearly that he accepts, and spends time with Zacchaeus and those around him. Zacchaeus the tax collector, despised, corrupt and a traitor, is turned into Zacchaeus the disciple – generous, full of integrity, willing to be seen and able to see Jesus properly.

LUKE 19:1-10

He entered Jericho and was passing through it. [2]A man was there named Zacchaeus; he was a chief tax collector and was rich. [3]He was trying to see who Jesus was, but on account of the crowd he could not, because he was short in stature. [4]So he ran ahead and climbed a sycamore tree to see him, because he was going to pass that way. [5]When Jesus came to the place, he looked up and said to him, 'Zacchaeus, hurry and come down; for I must stay at your house today.' [6]So he hurried down and was happy to welcome him. [7]All who saw it began to grumble and said, 'He has gone to be the guest of one who is a sinner.' [8]Zacchaeus stood there and said to the Lord, 'Look, half of my possessions, Lord, I will give to the poor; and if I have defrauded anyone of anything, I will pay back four times as much.' [9]Then Jesus said to him, 'Today salvation has come to this house, because he too is a son of Abraham. [10]For the Son of Man came to seek out and to save the lost.'

The importance of *seeing* grows as chapter 19 goes on. Jesus commandeers a donkey, and in fulfilment of the prophecy in Zechariah 9:9 rides into Jerusalem. The crowd see a coming Messiah, but the lens through which they see is one that is about political liberation and not spiritual change. There is a parallel with the problem of the Western economies in the run-up to 2008. When you measure wrongly and see badly, lies and deceit dominate the analysis of what is happening. The crowd are deeply disappointed by Jesus when his truth-filled reality turns out, a few days later, to be utterly different from their illusions about him. When Mammon rules us, we develop expectations that are false. We become disappointed, and we lash out in one way or another.

The Pharisees and the rulers see a problem. They do not know how to deal with this 'Messiah' whose aims are unclear to them, because they do not identify, as Luke says, 'the things that make for peace' (19:42). They assess Jesus wrongly, by the threat which they see to their interests, their strategies, to the stability of their power and influence in the complexities of Roman-occupied Jerusalem.

It is easy to judge them, but we do much the same. We allow our view of the world to be defined by what we measure, and most of the measuring is in the hands of Mammon. We do not identify the things that make for peace, but work on the calculation of risk and return, rather than abundance and generosity. Jesus sees truly, and seeing, gives freely, of forgiveness and of grace to those of no power, and also to those of power who have been corrupted but still seek to find a good way forward.

Are not most of us in one of these categories? Jesus sees the city very clearly, and sees its resistance and rebellion to the voice of God and the presence of its coming king. The disciples in Jerusalem see only an opportunity, the culmination of the mission. Jesus sees the trial that he will endure, and sees clearly the call of God that is his in Jerusalem, which will lead to his crucifixion.

How blind we often are to the realities of what is around us, especially when we cannot measure them. History is littered with those who wilfully or ignorantly close their eyes to what they cannot measure, or those who see falsely and measure badly, and do not see the threat that is posed. This comes from a fear of complexity, a hankering after simplicity even if it clouds more than it reveals. Nicholas Stern speaks eloquently of this problem in his recent book on the global response to climate change, *Why Are We Waiting?*[4]

He argues that accepting economic models that apply a price to a human life – for example based on income or consumption – gets us into great philosophical difficulties. It is surely more transparent and arguably more rigorous to analyse possible consequences on a number of dimensions, rather than to force an aggregation into a measure like GDP or aggregate consumption that buries some very problematic issues. Stern particularly argues that the environmental ecosystem is another highly relevant – indeed central – dimension. This broader approach may make simple-minded optimisation more difficult, but it follows from the nature of the issues at hand.

In other words, simple measures lead to overly simple solutions to the problems of life and ignore the parts that are unmeasurable. This has consequences, particularly when the unmeasurable is the call and will of God. The Pharisees were confining themselves to fairly simple analyses of what was happening in front of them, based on the value they placed on their power in the community, ignoring the values of the kingdom of God. The result was disaster from a direction they could not have expected at the time. They did not see that what was before them was the kingdom of God, and that its real but intangible impact was infinitely more important than their tangible power – the bricks and mortar of the city and temple – which seemed to them more real, and of greater value.

In contrast, Jesus sees with perfect clarity, because he sees with the eyes of the one who is in perfect fellowship with his Heavenly Father, and is perfectly filled with the Spirit of God. Nothing is missed. This divine 20/20 vision is our benchmark.

LUKE 19:45-8

Then he entered the temple and began to drive out those who were selling things there; [46]and he said, 'It is written,

"My house shall be a house of prayer";

but you have made it a den of robbers.'

[47]Every day he was teaching in the temple. The chief priests, the scribes, and the leaders of the people kept looking for a way to kill him; [48]but they did not find anything they could do, for all the people were spellbound by what they heard.

As the passage above shows, after his triumphal entry into Jerusalem, Jesus goes into the Temple. There he sees something which must have been to many an irritation, and to others a routine. The place is full of people buying and selling the necessities for sacrifice, and exchanging normal money for 'temple' money. As with all commercial environments, there will have been sharp practice in some areas, and integrity in others. But as seems to be the rule throughout history, bad money drives out good. Increasingly, the commercial activities of the temple had driven out those who were simply there to serve the needs of worshippers, and had marginalised those seeking to worship but lacking the financial means to do so.

This passage is well known, and is often quoted even by those who aren't Christians as an example of Jesus' 'righteous indignation'. Jesus sees into the hearts of those who are there and drives out their corruption.

The temple was a sacrament of the presence of God, a visible symbol of an invisible reality, built to draw people to transformed lives. It was doubtless costly to maintain, and there is no suggestion that somehow it should not have been maintained, or that it was improper to spend money to ensure that it was resourced. In fact, in the Old Testament, the book of the prophet Haggai makes quite the reverse point, that the financial cost of the temple and the demands of its rebuilding come ahead of people's own comfort, because it symbolises their commitment to the God of the temple.

But the rulers of the temple had lost sight of what it was there for, with their seeing dulled by long familiarity, and their hearing reduced by the clamour of money.

Is this too judgemental? It is easy to stand with the hindsight of 2,000 years, or the objectivity of not being in the financial markets, or in politics, and to see what we think they were doing wrong. Spectators are often better, in their own estimation, than the players. For those on the pitch there is noise, fast-moving action and exhaustion as well as the challenge from the other side.

To put it another way, most of us do not have to make the remarkably difficult decisions involved in economics or finance, whether as politicians or as those overseeing what happens. The power of Mammon is an immersion in a world whose frame of reference is set by Mammon.

T. H. White's book, *The Once and Future King* is a story about King Arthur. Its first part is called *The Sword in the Stone*, and was turned by Disney into a film in the 1960s. It was one of the delights of my childhood. In the book, Arthur, a servant boy, has a tutor, Merlin, a wizard. As part of what is called his 'eddication', he is turned into all kinds of animals, such as a fish, a hawk, an ant, a goose and a badger. The clever part of the story is that when he is a hawk he thinks like a hawk, and when he is a fish he cannot imagine the world above the water. His environment and nature set the limits of what he considers possible.

Jesus transforms what is possible. Because Jesus is God, there are no limits to possibility. The story of the incarnation – of God accepting the limits of human form – is the story of revealing the endless possibilities of God to human beings who, otherwise, see only limits. In Luke 19, the blind man is transformed by healing and follows Jesus. Zacchaeus has his personality transformed by meeting Jesus, and the hold of Mammon on his life is decisively broken.

The temple had been Mammonised. Once God's house, it was now under the occupation of a hostile power, not the Romans or even the rulers, but the spirit of Mammon. And Jesus drove Mammon out.

The poor, the powerful, and the institution at the very heart of Jewish national and religious life; all are changed. Luke 19 tells us that change is possible. The chapter is full of ambivalence, of sacrifice and hope. Luke, characteristically, does not tell the stories in easy ways with happy endings. They are deeply imbued with the complexities of life, and the consequences of the revolution that comes when we meet Jesus Christ.

The blind man follows Jesus, but we are not told what happens after Jesus' arrest. Did the disciples accept him?

Their false views and false measures were dethroned, the economically valueless was found to be of infinite value to God, but it is not stated whether this changed them to the degree that it should have done.

Zacchaeus would have been popular for a few days, but then, as the stories of the crucifixion reached Jericho, he would have been seen as a political liability.

The temple may well have gone back to its old ways, the disturbance of its cleansing a mere note in the duty officer's log.

Even these questions miss the point rather dramatically, because they are about outcomes and results. An annual performance review would have asked Jesus the tricky question: 'No doubt what you did was dramatic, symbolic and attention-gathering, but what was your strategy? What was your business case, and what were the outcomes?'

I am not against strategy, reviews and hard questions. Quite the reverse. But they do not dethrone Mammon. Dethroning requires the dramatic leap of faith of being defined by what we do not measure – cannot measure – because it is the infinitely valuable, utterly cosmos-transforming love of God in Jesus Christ. The step of faith made by the blind man, and by Zacchaeus; the right view that comes when we seek all that we need only and exclusively from Jesus: these are the moments of resolution that open our lives and our world to new possibilities, that set free the hope of humanity to be fully what it was created to be.

So how do we dethrone Mammon in our own lives, and in the lives of our communities and nations?

The answer must come through what we measure, what we see and what we hear. Everything is to be assessed through the eyes of Jesus.

What might God be calling you to value more?
What might God be calling you to value less?

3

What we have we hold

Key text *John 12*
Mary Anoints Jesus

Many rich people are very generous. They become philan-thropists and seek to give away a significant proportion of what they have. Of course it is a good and wonderful thing when the world's wealthy decide to share their fortune with the less fortunate, and of course many good and holy things have resulted from the philanthropists' chequebook. But the existence of philanthropy as a whole points to a more subtle way in which Mammon has captured our imag-ination. That is, the deception of Mammon is not simply to say that we need to hold on to everything we've got, but rather to say that what we've got is ours to dispose of as we choose.

Let me give you an example. A few years ago, in the UK, there was a small tax increase for people on the highest levels of income. Quite a number of those affected seemed to find the imposition of extra tax to be entirely unreason-able, describing it as socialist confiscation or 'worse than the Nazis'. A few went abroad, talking about the suffering of a tax exile being necessary to avoid the confiscatory nature of the oppressive system they found at home in the UK.

I did not know any of them personally, but I knew a little about them. Many were, and are still, philanthropists. They have set up foundations, and they give away money to very worthy causes. From their point of view, it is their money to give away.

By contrast, at the same time British forces were significantly engaged in Afghanistan. I came across some of them when they were back in the UK, not least when I took the funeral of a soldier who had been killed. It was profoundly moving. Listening to what his colleagues were saying (and independently of any view that anyone may have on the rights and wrongs of the intervention in Afghanistan) one heard underlined that what they held to be most precious – their own lives – was not to be held on to in the extreme circumstances of battle, if to hold on to it meant abandoning one's colleagues.

On the one hand, from people with the sort of wealth one can scarcely imagine, there was a sense that what we have, we hold. When we choose to use it or give it, it is our own sovereign choice as to what we do with it. On the other hand, these soldiers demonstrated to me a sense of 'what we have, we hold lightly'. And that came from people who were paid in a year probably less than the first group were paid in an hour.

I want to be clear that I am not judging the rich in this story. I have a feeling that if I were in their positon I might be likely to share their attitude. I have few illusions about my own capacity to stand entirely aside from the culture in which I live. All of us pick up the attitudes of those around us, of our friends, our family and our upbringing. But it becomes dangerous if we do not examine those attitudes properly. Nor am I saying that the second group, the soldiers, are in some sense saints. The ones I met were very normal human beings with some very exceptional qualities. So are many of the rich; yet I suggest that they have fallen into a trap.

What I am saying is that Mammon is a force that deceives and tricks us into attitudes that, when we look at them from the outside, are utterly wrong. In the first two chapters we have reflected on the false values that Mammon offers us as truth, and the challenge that Jesus sets before us with which to replace them. In this chapter, we are going to look at an underlying attitude to money which seeks to subvert the lie that Mammon sells us – that scarcity compels us to hold on to what we have – so that we can replace it with the truth of God, which is about extravagance and abundance.

Having looked at John 11 in the last but one chapter, let us move on to what happened almost immediately afterwards, in John 12. This is the story of Mary anointing Jesus' feet with precious ointment.

JOHN 12:1-11

Six days before the Passover Jesus came to Bethany, the home of Lazarus, whom he had raised from the dead. [2]There they gave a dinner for him. Martha served, and Lazarus was one of those at the table with him. [3]Mary took a pound of costly perfume made of pure nard, anointed Jesus' feet, and wiped them with her hair. The house was filled with the fragrance of the perfume. [4]But Judas Iscariot, one of his disciples (the one who was about to betray him), said, [5] 'Why was this perfume not sold for three hundred denarii and the money given to the poor?' [6](He said this not because he cared about the poor, but because he was a thief; he kept the common purse and used to steal what was put into it.) [7]Jesus said, 'Leave her alone. She bought it so that she might keep it for the day of my burial. [8]You always have the poor with you, but you do not always have me.'

[9]When the great crowd of the Jews learned that he was there, they came not only because of Jesus but also to see Lazarus, whom he had raised from the dead. [10]So the chief priests planned to put Lazarus to death as well, [11]since it was on account of him that many of the Jews were deserting and were believing in Jesus.

It is hard to exaggerate the ridiculous extravagance of what Mary does, and John puts it at the centre of the story in order for us to grasp the importance of the event.

Mary clearly has some savings, or may be quite a wealthy woman. It is possible, that, living in her own house, she has significant quantities of land and is able to derive a reasonable income from them. Whatever the case, whether the nard – the perfume – is all that she has ever saved or represents her pension, or whether it is something that she has been purchasing progressively (perhaps for her own anointing and funeral), it is vastly expensive. John's Gospel describes it as being worth 300 denarii. We know that an average labourer got one denarius for one day's work. So this is the thick end of a year's pay for an average male's work. In the UK today that would be the equivalent of over £25,000.

What is your most valuable possession?
Are there any circumstances under which you could
imagine giving it away?

This is not merely extravagant. To many of the onlookers it is an obscene waste. Jesus is alive. Very few there recognise the inevitability of what is going to happen to him, of where his journey to Jerusalem will end. The leaders in Jerusalem have just in the previous chapter set in motion their plan for Jesus' death. The raising of Lazarus was the last straw, even if the onlookers do not realise that. The leaders are determined to prove that Jesus is dangerous, defeatable and irrelevant to the future of the nation. All the emotions of the onlookers and disciples, the rulers and plotters, rest on the same worldview about how everything works: 'what we have we hold'. Their particular take may be that the nard should not be wasted, or that the stability of the political system should not be imperilled by wandering Galilean agitators, but all parties are united by this rule of life – 'what we have we hold'.

To follow Jesus as his disciple requires a shift of attitude that often overwhelms me. Most of us are utterly locked into the same way of thinking as the rich people I mentioned earlier in the chapter. We may criticise them, but we do so with an element of envy or *schadenfreude*. Jesus does not ask for an improvement in attitude, but for an entirely new worldview, based around his grace and sufficient love. Nothing is too much for him. His giving is more lavish and complete even than that of the soldiers I met.

Who cannot feel, when we contemplate that shift even for a moment, their hearts quail, as Mammon reminds us that we must hold what we have, and our hands clench instinctively around what we possess?

Perhaps through some prophetic inspiration, Mary understands what is happening, and who this Jesus is. Perhaps she is the only one who has realised and accepted that Jesus is going to die. Because she believes, she acts.

During the meal she breaks every rule in the place, and every convention of the time. First of all, she puts herself at the centre of events at a public dinner. As a woman in this ancient context, her role was to stay in the background and make sure the catering happened properly. Yet here she is, drawing attention to herself. Meals were held in public when they were important. People would come and watch. This is not a rude interruption to a small dinner party among friends, but a harsh and unwanted breach of decorum on a public occasion.

Second, abnormality turns to scandal when she touches Jesus' body, a man to whom she is neither married nor related. Some commentators have suggested that there is a considerable sense of sexual tension in the room. Onlookers must have been wondering whether she was offering more than the nard.

Third, she replaces the smell of the death of Lazarus with the smell of the perfume for anointing the body of Jesus for his own burial. When that comes, less than a week later, there will not be time to anoint him, so she does it now.

The question is this: why does Mary break the rules? Or perhaps more specifically, why does Jesus praise Mary at the

end of this story? It is because, in this story at least, Mary
sees through the eyes of God. She demonstrates the extent
of the change of heart and view to which we are called. A
favourable view of Mary is often that she demonstrates love.
In Johannine terms this is far more than that. It is a Sign.
Unbelief is confronted by one who believes, and for once the
one who believes is not Jesus. Mary, in John 11, has been
called to believe: now she believes and demonstrates her
belief not merely in service and worship, but by exchanging one worldview – of scarcity – for another, of abundance.
The life of Lazarus, sitting at the table, has been restored.
That is not only a cause of indescribable joy; for Mary the
world has clicked into a new shape, with new rules, new
attitudes, new possibilities. Lazarus sits next to Jesus; she
lives in the new order of things.

Her action reveals that she alone sees the course that life
will take for Jesus, and for the world, as he moves towards
Good Friday. What is more, her action reveals the nature
of God: she has emptied herself – given everything – just
as the merchant did with the pearl of great value,[1] and
just as Jesus will do on Good Friday. It is not only that,
among all the disciples, Mary is the one to demonstrate
love and faithfulness; also, through her, we discover what
God is really like.

As Mary pours £25,000 worth of perfume over Jesus' feet,
she replaces the ugliness of the fate that awaits him, and the
tension of the murder plot overshadowing him, with a gift of
beauty, and a scent that pervades the whole house.[2]

Mary's act is one of worship, and worship is how we tackle
the deceiving effect of Mammon, which corrupts and distorts

the way in which we look at what we have, so that what we have we hold as though it were ours.

The reaction of the onlookers is predictable. Most are deeply uncomfortable. Only one, Judas, expresses the discomfort, but the story gives a clear impression that he is merely vocalising the inner thoughts of many there: 'What a waste!'

To what have you reacted by saying or thinking, 'What a waste!'?
Reflect on that experience. What, to you,
made it wasteful?

How often have we said that? We look at some historic act that facilitates worship, like the building of a church, or the donation of money for inspirational art, or we look at a life that has been wholly given to Christ in some remarkable way, and some of us, or some part of us, wonders, 'What else could that money have paid for?' or 'What else could that person have done in the world?'

Years ago, a friend of mine was asked to a party at which there was a famous and extremely wealthy man, now long dead. My friend was a clergyman but was in a shirt and tie, rather than his usual clerical shirt and collar. He had spent much of his life working in areas of great deprivation and poverty, serving the poor and building up community. He was exceptionally talented, and a first-class athlete to boot. The wealthy man chatted to him for quite a while, obviously enjoying his company. Then he asked, 'And what do you do?' My friend replied, 'I'm a clergyman.' The wealthy man replied, 'What a waste!', and walked away.

It is not only the rich who feel like this. I alluded in the last chapter to the beginning, in 2015, of the first year of the Community of St Anselm at Lambeth Palace, a quasi-monastic programme for ten months for people from around the world aged between twenty and thirty-five. Out of hundreds of applications, we picked around thirty-five, sixteen living in community and twenty outside, continuing with their daily lives.

What else does the world consider wasteful?
What value might God see in those things?

The residents, and the non-residents to the extent to which it is possible, spend their time in a combination of prayer, learning, serving the poor and self-examination. For some reason the Community attracted much attention, and some people asked if it was really a good idea. The participants have had their capacity for economic activity diminished. They are focused on God. If the Church ever sees any benefit it will be in several decades' time, and quite possibly on the other side of the world. Surely, this bunch of exceptionally talented and quite brilliant people could do better than spend ten months in the emotional rigours of an intentional community? What a waste!

The Community of St Anselm is finding in practice that God's economics do not work in that way. Like Mary they have poured out a year's pay, and much more in terms of discomfort and the demand on their lives, for the sake of Christ. The result is that even now the benefits are felt. Prayer is more and more at the centre of the life of Lambeth Palace. When the Anglican Primates (the leaders of each Province of the Anglican Communion) met in January 2016, the community were there praying for them. In a mission in the Diocese of Canterbury, they were active participants. Economic value was disregarded and, in God's economy, a new spirit of worship and witness abounds, lavishly, even extravagantly.

It is significant that the criticism of waste comes through Judas, because in John's Gospel, Judas exemplifies betrayal and selfishness. Mammon has deceived Judas, who is described as the treasurer to the disciples. He holds the money-bag (and steals from it), and is the most involved with the finances. He is described elsewhere as a zealot, a radical who is seeking to overthrow the Roman domination of Israel. One gets the impression of a man who was focused on making sure 'the main thing remained the main thing', to use some management jargon.

Mammon does not trick many of us into being Scrooge. Few people end up overtly worshipping money, and being so utterly obsessed with its possession that they would sacrifice their own comfort, all relationships, any popularity, and all fullness of life to its service. Money creates few monks whose worship and duty is solely to Mammon.

But Mammon does deceive in terms of value, and in terms of right thinking about the nature of the world in which we live.

Judas' reputation precedes him. And therefore it can be easy for us to distance ourselves from his mistake. Since we're not (we think) as bad as Judas, surely we wouldn't have reacted like Judas had we been present for Mary's extraordinary act. But Judas' reaction in this story is, at a gut-level, very understandable. Which of us would not have this reaction?

It is even within the realm of possibility that Judas had good intentions. John tells us that Judas sees the potential for selling the nard and giving the money to the poor (although, ever eager to convince us of Judas's guilt, he adds that that was not his genuine concern). Notwithstanding the fact that Judas was using his protest as a purely political statement, to undermine and criticise the work of Mary, it is something that many of us can imagine saying today. Judas may be seen to illustrate the most natural reactions of each of us under circumstances of pressure.

When have you heard yourself questioning the value
of another's worship?
What scandalised you about it, and what can you
learn from your reaction?

It is worth pausing here and considering the story again, from the viewpoint of Judas. There is probably quite a lot of anger in him already, not least from his guilty conscience about stealing money. He is trying to justify what he does as being for the greater good, to further the cause he serves. He was surely calculating the odds of a successful week; of Jesus getting to where he was obviously going, triggering full-scale revolution. Money is fuel for such an enterprise, so where will resources be found? Now here is this fool of a woman risking Jesus' reputation, and the success of what Judas sees as their mission, by throwing away such wealth. What a waste! Reading Judas sympathetically and imaginatively we too find ourselves impatient with a merely symbolic act, contemptuous of ineffective emotion, and fearful about a disastrous loss of focus.

As someone who struggles to escape being too task-focused I can easily see why he reacted as he did.

Jesus, as usual, replies with a sentence that can be misunderstood and taken out of context, but which goes to the very heart of the matter. Jesus says: 'You will always have the poor among you, but you do not always have me' (John 12:8).

How do you shape your life in order that worship
of Jesus comes first?

As in so much of John's Gospel, Jesus' words are about himself. It is one of those moments which provokes C. S. Lewis, in his book *Mere Christianity*, into commenting that the kind of self-centredness it displays is either indefensible, or a demonstration that Jesus is who he says he is.

What Mary has done can now be seen in a completely different light. The onlookers saw it as extravagant and deeply embarrassing, without much purpose. Jesus restates it as prophetic. Jesus shows us that Mary's act points to his death and to its cosmic significance. As such, it is an act of worship. Jesus' claim to be worshipped overrides all other claims. Worship is the way in which we say that the centre of the whole cosmos is not ourselves, or our society, or anyone else, but God. Worship does not so much undermine the deceptions of Mammon as obliterate them. Their dark influence on our lives is eliminated in the bright flash of the reality of Jesus as God himself. Mary 'gets' that, and in getting it she acts appropriately.

In Judas and Mary, we see embodied two competing economic systems: Judas represents the economy of
Mammon, and Mary represents the economy of God, the
economy of 'manna'.[3] Judas sees people and objects in material terms according to their monetary value, whereas Mary
sees people and objects as precious gifts from God, thus to
be cherished. Judas represents an economy of scarcity. His
fundamental assumption is that there is not enough to go
around, which is to say that Judas' disposition is one of fear,
and fear produces an anxiety to control. In this passage, Judas
tries to exercise control on multiple fronts. Not only does
he attempt to control how the disciples use their money, but
he also tries to govern the manner in which Mary relates to
Jesus. Judas believes power is predicated on regulation and
management.

Mary, on the other hand, is decidedly out of control in this
story. She is not concerned with anything but Jesus. She is
not concerned with efficiency, or thrift, or measurement, or
appearances. Mary embarrasses herself. She goes completely
overboard. But she does so because she lives within an economy of abundance – where God's provision of manna in the
wilderness far exceeds the Israelites' hunger and their capacity to harvest it (see Exodus 16:1-35). Spending money on
Jesus and helping the poor are not mutually exclusive, because
in the world that God has created there is always enough to
go around. The value of things is determined not by their
monetary value, but by their relationship to Jesus. In short,
everything – including all the nard in the world – exists *for*
Jesus. Mary assumes that there is enough nard in the world
for God to accomplish everything God wants to accomplish

with it, whether or not she uses her whole bottle. Judas is defined by what he has. Mary is defined by how she gives. Mary has true power. She is not in control of the disciples' common purse, but she is the one in the story who has the power to do something extraordinary.

So with all these deceptions coming from Mammon, how do we dethrone the myth that what we have we hold? It generates a powerful stream of subconscious ideas in our society today. It relies very heavily on fear, and much of our politics draws on that fear. Fear is a powerful tool of Mammon. So we are taught to fear the outsider and the stranger, especially the needy stranger. Fear has a crippling effect on any country or society. It encourages extremism and populism in politics. It establishes a hermeneutic of suspicion, a way of looking at the world which begins all relationships with the question 'What are they trying to get out of me?', or 'What power are they seeking to acquire?'

The UK remains among the top eight most prosperous nations on earth, with military who are powerful, trained and effective at defending us both here and abroad. We are a major exporter of traded goods as well as commercial services. We have not had a revolution or *coup d'état* since 1745, and no successful one since 1688. For centuries, our politics has been – albeit, by today's standards, corrupt, venal, narrow-minded and unacceptable – a model of moderation compared to the majority of the rest of the world. The United Kingdom has more to be grateful for, has received more, and, for that matter, given more to the world than many other and larger countries. Our culture, especially our literature, art, music and theatre, remains outstanding. We have a national health service which may have failings – as all large institutions do – but is an extraordinary gift to anyone who is ill, and delivers without ever asking the patient to pay the bill. Our children can be well educated for free. Our universities rank among the best in the world.

This is not to say that in the UK all is for the best in the best of all possible worlds. Of course, there is a huge amount that could be improved. We do not want to see rough sleepers on the streets. That is a scandal that should be tackled, and can be, as we have proved in the past. We do not want people to be dependent on food banks, and any unemployment is a curse and a denial of God's purposes for the human being. Poverty, even relative poverty, is a tragedy. Depression, family breakdown, substance abuse and crime stain many lives. But it is an extraordinary privilege to live in this country, with its freedoms and protections.

Compared to any period in history, and certainly compared to the huge majority of people alive in the world today, we are exceptionally fortunate. But at the time of writing, in the early part of 2016, with various political campaigns going on in the UK and abroad, anyone would think that everything we have is about to collapse around us. The campaigns by both sides in the referendum on European Union member-ship have been based on 'what we have we hold'. They have sought support by arguing that there is more risk, more danger, more to be feared, on the other side of the argu-ment. The absence of any positive, soul-stirring vision has been striking.

When I look across the Atlantic at some of the campaigning going on for the 2016 US presidential election, again so much of it seems to be based on fear, failure and an absence of hope. All such fear is the tool of Mammon, who, like Judas, looks at any extravagant giving or sense of abundance, and grumbles and moans that this is all going to be a disaster. Mammon causes us to embrace fear, and fear drives us to selfishness, and to grasping what we hold ever more tightly.

I remember a friend of mine who worked as a lawyer specialising in divorce. One of his clients was the wife of a very wealthy man, who had declared his wealth to the court at a sum far less than the reality, in order to reduce the divorce settlement. Suspecting this was the case, my friend asked the wife if she had any idea what the true figure was. To his astonishment she gave the precise value of his easily available wealth, apart from the house, with great accuracy, as of the week when she had been asked to leave the house. She knew this because her husband's main occupation, once a week, was to calculate his personal wealth, in order to enjoy the sense of how much he had.

While he sat counting what he had, something that was of far greater value – his marriage – was slipping away from him. To echo a previous chapter, since he could not measure it, it did not define him. He could not count it, so he did not value it. Yet he valued, and was defined by, his money. Mammon had deceived that man into calculating everything on the basis of Mammon's values, not those of Jesus Christ.

So how do we challenge Mammon's lie that 'what we have we hold'? How do we go about noticing the manna that God lavishes daily upon his people? We begin with worship. Worship comes in many forms, but at its heart is centring our whole attention on God found through Jesus Christ. It is about seeing the act of worship not as a tool to improve ourselves, but as a good end in and of itself. The wonderful thing about worship is that it is not 'for' anything; it is not a means to some useful end. In that rather narrow sense it is without purpose: worship is a good in itself. It requires from us an attitude that looks to God, not for a result but as the object of our entire adoration.

Mary's act of worship towards Jesus does not have any purpose. His feet are not better as a result of the anointing of nard – in fact, whatever he was sitting on probably got covered in nard as well – and the worship will not prevent his death, nor for that matter have any impact on those around him. But it is an act of worship, so it is good.

In the first chapter, I wrote about Cardinal Văn Thuận, and his celebrating of mass every day with one grain of rice and enough rice wine to hold in the palm of the hand. Mammon challenges us, 'What does that do?' It did not alleviate his aloneness. It did not result in his prison sentence being shorter. It did not make his beatings and torture less severe. It was simply worship. It was the saying of words over a minute piece of carbohydrate, the nearest he could find to bread and wine, so that his heart was constantly turned outwards to Jesus.

Worship has at its heart the offering of beauty, the beauty of ourselves made in the image of God, rather than the focus on ourselves as that which we have and to which we intend to hold.

It is for this reason that offerings of worship are so good in and of themselves. It may be the offering of time alone, at the beginning or end of the day, or during the day – whenever

suits us best – in which we spend time declaring, in whatever way we choose (more on that in a moment), the beauty
and love of God as we know him in Christ. We can use
set prayers and liturgies, easily findable on the web, or in
prayer books. For the tech-savvy, the Church of England
and others have even produced apps. We can pray extem-
porarily, spending time with Scripture declaring the
wonders of God. We can sit in quiet and adoring silence,
allowing the presence of God to fill our lives and our hearts
to turn away from themselves towards God. We can contemplate some art or poetry which draws us to God, rejoicing
in the insight it brings.

I remember visiting Venice, and going to one of the mu-
seums where there was a series of paintings by Tintoretto of
the crucifixion. As I looked at them, to this day I can remember the love that welled up in me for the Jesus who had
suffered so much on my account. Nobody could claim that
the pictures in the museum were accomplishing much; they
were simply there. We would not pretend that Tintoretto was
himself a saint. I am emphatically not an art expert in any
way at all, especially when it comes to paintings or the visual
arts. Yet, the beauty of the painting inspired in me a sense of
worship which was a good in itself. As a result, it set me more
firmly on the path of following Jesus.

A powerful example of the effect that worship of Jesus
Christ has on how we see the world was evident in the actions
of a number of Coptic Christians from a poor village in the
south of Egypt who, in 2015, were brutally executed on a
beach in Libya by a group linked to the so-called Islamic State,
also known as Daesh.

The Copts could have escaped death by turning away from their Christian faith, or at least pretending to. Yet they would not. They died crying out prayers to Jesus Christ and worshipping his name. One can imagine how many people would say, 'What a waste!' It is absurd and wasteful to throw away life in such a way when you could have held on to it, simply by saying a few words from which you could very easily have recanted. Instead, lives that originated from lovemaking and blossomed into children playing as they grew up in their small villages, lives defined by relationships and full of depth, ended in pain and humiliation on a beach at the hands of brutal enemies. What a waste? Not at all! By rejecting the idea that they must hold on to what they had, they offered in worship all that there was for them to give, and in doing so transformed that act of murder from deep darkness to an example of the brightest light in humanity.

The transformation of our understanding – what Paul in Romans 12:2 calls the renewing of our minds – is so decisive in how we live and in how we think that it can only be done from outside ourselves, by the impact of the Spirit of God. Mary saw in a different way once she had seen the reality of the life of Christ. In worship, as we meet with God, we are changed.

One of the great insights of Catholic Social Teaching is solidarity. In the 1980s, the word was adopted as the title of the Polish Trade Union movement, *Solidarność*, in its struggle against the communist regime. By the end of the 1980s, in Berlin, Leipzig and across what was then East Germany, churches met for prayer, and people came in huge numbers. As they prayed for freedom they were bound together in solidarity.

In the Community of St Anselm, as we pray we find unity. The work of the Spirit of God is to integrate, to make whole and bring us together. We are changed as we recognise more deeply that we belong together, rich or poor, from all sorts of different backgrounds and worldviews. The Spirit transforms, and what we have we hold, but what we have is utterly changed. We hold to a sense of the common good, of belonging to one another, which makes that holding part of God's economy of generosity and abundance.

So, let us first restore worship as an end in itself to the centre of our being and our existence. Let us say to ourselves that a day without worship is a day wasted, and worse than that, a day in which for a moment we permit Mammon to override manna – to convince us that what we have materially we hold for our individual selves alone.

Second, there must be an appropriate and extravagant generosity in the way in which we live our lives. We dethrone Mammon with lifestyle. Dethroning is a practice of life, not an instant decision. We need to set in place dethroning habits so that instinctively we act as those who have dethroned. Worship gives a new worldview, and a determination to follow a lifestyle turns the worldview into a mode of being.

On what things might God be calling you to loosen your grip?
What 'dethroned habits' have you witnessed in others?
How would these actions make a difference to you and those around you?

Mammon's deception is not only about money, but also creeps into so many other areas in life. Mammon is ultimately and utterly materialist, and works with all that we see and feel and know and touch materially. Mammon tells us to hold on to things – to family, to home, to career – and in so doing, takes the gifts of God which these things are, and twists them subtly into chains that hold us in slavery before Mammon's throne.

Of these, especially within the Western Church, family can easily become the greatest idol that we have. As a parish priest, if you want to have a bit of controversy after a morning service, preach on the family, and say that Christ must come before family. They are not in opposition necessarily, but can easily become so. One often hears people say, 'Nothing comes before my family.'

Yet, Jesus says that anyone who loves family more than him is not worthy of the kingdom of God. The New Testament sets out the family as one of the base communities not only of society and the state, but also of the Church. It is often a sort of mini-Church, the Church in microcosm, in which we are able to live as community, learning not to be centred entirely on ourselves, but caring for others who need us and whom we also need.

Of course I am not only talking about the nuclear family, because there are many who do not live in a family with a partner and children, but about the extended family, that network which consists of those who have a link to us by nature or nurture and are the objects of our compassion and concern, of our celebration and service, in a particular way.

Yet when such a group, and especially the nuclear family, becomes a sort of god, which we worship with all that we have – time, energy and money – at the cost of anything beyond, then Mammon has succeeded. Instead, extravagant generosity around the family consists in creating communities of celebration and abundance, in which the outsider, the alien and the stranger are welcomed and where they find healing, hope and company because of the self-giving of the family. It is a conscious using of the strength that a good family provides to ensure that we are able to be more other-centred. I am certainly not suggesting that we neglect the family, or take it for granted, but rather that we celebrate all that it gives us in the way we behave towards others, and learn from its experience of community what it is to be with others.

The same is true of career. Ambition is excellent, but not if it is guided by Mammon. The unavailing struggle to ensure that we leave a mark and are remembered in some way is addressed powerfully in the Old Testament in Ecclesiastes.[4] The writer – in Hebrew, Qoheleth, or 'the preacher' – has a bleak view of a world in which the cycle of life repeats and all human striving is vanity, seeking after the wind. All our ambitions, for career, for family, for children and grandchildren, are to have Christ at the centre and Mammon dethroned; to recognise God's abundant manna and to share it in the conviction that there is plenty for everyone. Mary's gift is to trust that an offering to God is, of itself, of lasting memory and beauty.

This upside-down valuing, God-shaped economics, is why Jean Vanier sees infinite value in those with learning difficulties. They are remembered before God, and so in solidarity and sacrifice he has put Mammon off the throne and Christ at the heart of life. Like Mary, he imitates God and for that reason alone, he will be held forever in God's heart.

Finally, remember that in John 12, Jesus is at a party. They were celebrating the life of Lazarus. It was not a time of mourning and sadness, but rather one of joy and companionship. Mammon is dethroned by the celebration of the eternal and of the Truth, by the relishing of those things which we neither see, nor measure, but which are transforming of the quality of our lives, of friendship, of life, of liberty and hope.

We used to have an annual slogan in my parish church, to give us some priorities for the year. It was a struggle to think of new ones until we found one that kept us going happily year after year: 'more parties, less meetings'.[5] It sounded frivolous, but at its heart it said that we are a community, not a corporation; we are a family, not an organisation.

Mary, in her prophetic inspiration, points us to the abundance of Christ. Because God provides manna, we can party even in the wilderness. In doing so, Mammon – who tells us that there is never enough to go round, and what we have we must hold – is dethroned.

Do you remember a time when someone acted in
a surprisingly selfless manner to your benefit?
Do you remember a time when you acted in that way?
Have you ever regretted it?

4

What we receive we treat as ours

Key text *John 13*
Jesus washes the disciples' feet

Money and power are closely related. It is almost impossible to see the impact of one without understanding the desire for the other. Power flows to a large degree from money. And money is easier to acquire when one has power. One of the characteristics of poverty is that you are the object of other people's power, rather than the subject who decides what to do with your own power. In the nineteenth century, a rich man would be described as 'being of independent means'. He controlled his own affairs. One of the greatest acts of empowering women in England was the Married Women's Property Act 1882, which changed the law so that married women could own and dispose of property in their own right. This gave a level of independence to women who had their own money, which had previously applied only to single women or widows. Financial independence gave rise to more power.

How we handle power will therefore have a huge impact on how we handle money. The problem is that what we receive we treat as ours. There is nothing new about that. In 1 Corinthians 4:7 Paul asks the church in Corinth: 'For who sees anything different in you? What do you have that you did not receive? And if you received it, why do you boast as if it were not a gift?'

A Swiss friend of mine, who gave up a life in politics and the law to become a hermit and now leads a remarkable religious community, often says *'c'est tout grâce'* (it's all grace): what we receive is a gift that we have not earned and for which we must account. We are stewards. At the heart of Christian discipleship is to know that all we have is gift, and to live out that knowledge. To understand that 'it's all grace' is to know that what we receive is the providence of God: God's love freely given in tangible forms.

That may sound exaggerated. If someone has strived and worked, invented and developed, built up a business, made their money, surely it is theirs to dispose of as they please. After all, they have earned it. Even Jesus sometimes seems to say that, as in Matthew 20:1-16. In Jesus' parable, a man hires labourers at various points during the day, and pays them all the same, however long they have worked. The ones who have worked all day protest, but the landlord answers, 'Am I not allowed to do what I choose with what belongs to me?' What we receive we may use, but what we receive is still gift. The successful businessperson has their intelligence, their skills, their health only through the grace of God. Everything fundamentally depends on God.

Do you consider yourself to be a powerful person?
Over what do you have power? In what do you not have power?
What do you usually use your power for?

JOHN 13:1-11

Now before the festival of the Passover, Jesus knew that his hour had come to depart from this world and go to the Father. Having loved his own who were in the world, he loved them to the end. [2]The devil had already put it into the heart of Judas son of Simon Iscariot to betray him. And during supper [3]Jesus, knowing that the Father had given all things into his hands, and that he had come from God and was going to God, [4]got up from the table, took off his outer robe, and tied a towel around himself. [5]Then he poured water into a basin and began to wash the disciples' feet and to wipe them with the towel that was tied around him. [6]He came to Simon Peter, who said to him, 'Lord, are you going to wash my feet?' [7]Jesus answered, 'You do not know now what I am doing, but later you will understand.' [8]Peter said to him, 'You will never wash my feet.' Jesus answered, 'Unless I wash you, you have no share with me.' [9]Simon Peter said to him, 'Lord, not my feet only but also my hands and my head!' [10]Jesus said to him, 'One who has bathed does not need to wash, except for the feet, but is entirely clean. And you are clean, though not all of you.' [11]For he knew who was to betray him; for this reason he said, 'Not all of you are clean.'

When we come to Chapter 13 of John's Gospel, the foundation of the story is that Jesus 'knowing that the Father had given all things into his hands, and that he had come from God and was going to God ...' washes his disciples' feet. It is the *knowing* that enables the action to take place. What he had received – authority, power, the blessing of God in all that he did, his intimacy with the Father – is set aside because he knew that all came from God. He 'did not regard equality with God as something to be exploited' (Philippians 2:6), but was prepared for it to be emptied out, for love of the Father.

The more we look at the person of Jesus, especially around the time of his passion and death, the more we see the immense reversal of attitude that is required when we become his disciples. It is rather encouraging that his disciples did not seem any better at handling this reversal than we are. To treat as mine what I receive is viewed as the natural or correct order of things in our society, to such an extent that any other approach has radical political connotations. Public ownership of the means of production is a left-wing approach, with its roots in the work of Karl Marx. Much of Marx's approach, both in *The Communist Manifesto* and in *Das Kapital*, is asking what happens to the surplus value of a person's labour. Do they keep what they receive? Is it theirs? Or does it go to the owners of the company for which they work? Marx famously begins *The Communist Manifesto* with the words, 'Workers of the world, unite! You have nothing to lose but your chains.'

His answer was common ownership of the means of production, or wholesale nationalisation as we might call it. It failed, of course, because it did not take into account a vast range of factors, from the economic (such a process has tended to lead to centralised, inefficient and totalitarian bureaucracies), to the ethical (he did not either accept or, therefore, address the basic sinfulness of human beings).

Sin holds on to things, making 'it's mine' out of a gift. In J. R. R. Tolkien's famous books *The Hobbit* and *The Lord of the Rings*, the holder of a golden ring acquires great power. The ring comes to each holder in different ways: by theft, by murder, by chance; but for each person the power they receive becomes the dominant factor in their lives, and causes their death if they do not dispose of the ring. It has the potential for infinite good or evil, but its corrosive effect invariably leads to the latter. The ring is 'My Precious', and those possessing it will turn even against their friends to hold on to it.

St Benedict, in his Rule for monks, sees with immense clarity the bad effect it has on a community if we treat as ours everything we receive. He insists, again and again, that monks should have no private possessions at all. More than that, anything any individual receives as a gift has to be given to the community. It is clear that this was always a big problem. Even bigger, though, was the inequality caused by private possessions that, in the hierarchical societies of the Middle Ages, would provoke deep divisions within the community.

Not to hold on to what we receive – even to accept that it is not ours to use – goes against all our instincts. Only the Holy Spirit of God can so change us that we are ready to see that what we have is a trust, something to be held for the benefit of others.

How were possessions and power treated in your family of origin?
How do you treat them now and how do you
account for the difference, if any?
What and / or who has informed your current perspective?

If this is difficult at an individual level, how much more difficult it is at the level of society. Before any government budget is announced, every lobby for every interest group pleads for more money. Even those who are wealthy resist anything which reduces income, however marginally. For example, there are regular debates in the UK over the income level at which social security benefits should taper off, or even whether they should be means-tested at all. Those at the higher end of the income spectrum are often vocal in their opposition to any changes that would see them lose out on benefits they have received, for example child benefit payments.

In Catholic Social Teaching, there is a foundational principle of the universal destination of goods: that the wealth of the world is given by God for the benefit of every person in the world. To amass an unfair proportion is thus to deprive others. It calls for a vision of God that overcomes, in its beauty and generosity, the innate selfishness of our societies.

One of the most beautiful things we have to understand about the love of God is that in what we receive there is freedom to serve others, to ensure a world without extremes of deprivation. To see what we own as being for others is to experience freedom. Not to do so is to open our eyes to fear.

Chapter 13 of John's Gospel tells a story about power, and indirectly about wealth. Jesus has gathered his disciples in the Upper Room for a meal, anticipating the coming Passover festival, during which they will commemorate the liberation of the Israelites from slavery in Egypt. It is the greatest feast of the Jewish calendar, which means that as a rabbi, Jesus was the centre of attention among those who followed him. People followed Jesus around Judea and Galilee to hear

his teaching throughout his whole ministry. Here, his closest followers were hanging on to his every syllable. Jesus is
their leader. He holds authority and power in this group, and
everyone is keen to see how he will wield it in this moment.
What will the rabbi's Passover sermon be this year?

In fact, the anticipation the disciples felt was even more
intense than that. Most of them had come to the conclusion
that Jesus was not just any rabbi, but the promised Messiah,
the one sent from God to draw the people of Israel back to
freedom, to hope and to independence. The Passover was
therefore particularly resonant. The disciples were aware of
the crisis which was breaking, that the leaders were plotting
against Jesus, so there must have been a sense that a great miracle was about to occur, and that the liberation of Israel was
at hand. Furthermore, here the disciples found themselves as
the intimate friends and followers of this Messiah, who would
lead the revolution. Thus, power and influence, wealth and
security beckoned. Raised from poverty and insignificance in
the far north of Israel, they could see before them a place in
history, a legacy, and doubtless a dynasty enriched by their
decision to follow Jesus through hardship and difficulty over
the previous three years.

Jesus does not deny that he has power and authority, though
he has not sought that power for power's sake. His power
comes from being faithful to the will of his Father. He is absolutely certain about his mission and his calling. As the opening
verses of John 13 say, he knows from whom he has come,
what he has to do and where he is going. He rests in the assur-
ance of being one with the Father, utterly at the centre of the
will of God. He is indeed truly the only entirely free person

in that Upper Room. He need not prove anything, he does not desire anything, except to obey his Father. What will Jesus do with his power?

He does something that no one expects or anticipates. Jesus subverts the whole notion of power and leadership, by taking the role of a servant. Removing his outer clothes, he takes a towel, and washes the feet of his disciples. Jesus takes all those anxious anticipations, all those watchful eyes and eager ears, and turns things upside down. He does not give a rousing speech or draw out battle plans. Right before their eyes, the disciples see the God who created the whole world – the God who is all-knowing and almighty, and for whom nothing is impossible – decide that he will rescue Israel and the world by taking on the form of a servant. The most powerful being in the universe kneels down to wash someone's dirty feet. This is the radical reversal at the heart of Christianity. When the one to whom all power was given knelt down to wash feet, God reversed the world order. Jesus showed us that power in this world is not really what you think. It's not money, or status, or beauty. True power lies in washing feet, in taking up the role of a servant.

At the beginning of 2016, on the last day of a meeting with the Primates of the Anglican Communion (the chief archbishops or bishops of the provinces of the Anglican family of churches around the world), we gathered for a closing communion service. It was a memorable scene. We sat together in the crypt of Canterbury Cathedral, the stones around us full of the prayers, petitions, joys and sufferings of 800 years of Christian life. Within these walls, Archbishop Thomas Becket had been murdered in 1170, and his body brought into this Crypt. The great Renaissance philosopher and theologian Erasmus had prayed in the chapel where we sat. It has been a centre for the prayer of archbishops, of leaders of the nation, and even of one pope.

The altar was set for communion. On one side was the crosier (the crook bishops carry as a sign they are shepherds of the people) of St Gregory – Pope Gregory the Great. It was he who, in the sixth century, had sent St Augustine as the first Archbishop of Canterbury, to reclaim Britain for the Christian faith. The crosier had been lent by the Monastery of San Gregorio in Rome as a sign of their identification with the efforts of the Primates to avoid division within the Anglican Communion. The loan symbolised our links to Rome, stretching over 1,400 years, and reminded us that millions – possibly tens of millions – of people around the globe were praying for the meeting. On the other side of the altar was an object of similar age, the Gospel book, beautifully illuminated, which was brought by Augustine himself to England when he arrived in 597, lent for the occasion by Corpus Christi College, Cambridge. This second symbol reminded us of the Scriptures, the word of God, which have guided God's people from age to age, which still serve as our principal and overriding authority, constantly reinterpreted generation by generation, but continually pointing us back to the Christ to whom they refer.

Thus, before us were three objects: crosier, altar and Gospels, drawing us back to our history, to our call to be shepherds and to love the sheep, to our obedience to the revelation of God in Jesus Christ, and to the present moment of communion with one another.

And before the altar sat our preacher for the day, Jean Vanier, a man in his late eighties, who, from a distinguished background, has spent his life living with those with learning difficulties and disability, forming communities around the world where they are respected and loved, living as equals alongside those without such challenges. One could say without exaggeration that, within the Christian faith, he has been the primary agent through whom God has transformed the Church's approach to those with disability, moving us from ignorance and fear, through tolerance, to respecting them now as human beings of absolutely equal value to everyone else. That journey from fear to respect is itself a retreat from Mammon, because it says that the economic output of an individual is not the source of their value. Their value comes from God himself.

Jean Vanier spoke to us from this text, John 13. Then the Primates washed each other's feet, as a reminder of our call to follow Christ, who did not hold on to power but made himself a slave, emptying himself of everything, even unto death on a cross. The action of washing each other's feet with tears, prayers and blessings set the pattern for the rest of the celebration of the Eucharist. It was a moment of transformation.

Every Primate in the chapel had been given power and, to some extent, wealth or access to wealth greater than many others in their home Province. In many areas (including the UK), there is prestige and respect accorded to those holding such a position. It is a heady mix, which is easily inhaled, leading to a sense of self-importance. More than that, being from many different cultures, speaking different languages, having different experiences, our lives had built natural barriers between us. Additionally, the history of our nations is filled with deeply tragic episodes. The UK had dominated the countries of many of those there through colonial oversight and imperialistic aggression. Some could remember what it meant to be ruled by another nation. There were profound differences of view on such areas as the right way to regard human sexuality, and deep resentments existed.

The Primates are not especially bad. On the contrary, my experience of them has been of a very deep generosity, a profound spirituality and a sense of collegial love among us. Yet, so often, even the strength of Christian commitment can be overwhelmed by issues of personality, politics and history. Walls had been built by worldly power and by human greed in previous generations. The symbolic and yet deeply meaningful act of washing the feet of the other Primates was for each of us a way of breaking down these walls.

The question remains, however, whether one-off acts of that sort can ever become something deeper and more influential in our everyday conduct. How can they become 'dethroning habits'? How can the pressures which, in the case of the Primates, began to press in on them as soon as they left the meeting, be resisted, indeed overcome by the generosity and love of Christ?

When Jesus washes his disciples' feet, it makes them deeply uncomfortable. Peter seeks to avoid the discomfort by refusing to have his feet washed. Even more then than now, the sight of a leader humbling himself before those who are meant to follow them is one that raises considerable tension. I quite recently experienced the discomfort caused when a perceived 'leader' does not behave as expected. Returning from a journey, I arrived at Victoria Station in London and took the bus to my home, a flat on the upper floor of Lambeth Palace. As we were setting off, two people I knew got on and I greeted them. When we arrived and got off the bus, I took my suitcase. They were deeply shocked and very uncomfortable, trying to take it from me. One warned me seriously that if I was seen carrying my own suitcase in their home country, I would lose all respect.

On a vastly different and more significant scale, Pope Francis has occasioned much criticism by his preference for simplicity, in the liturgy he uses, in his lifestyle, and in his service. He has changed the layout of the grand room where he welcomes official guests so that he sits at the same level as his visitor, rather than on a dais above them. For some, this indicates a lack of respect for his office. It is, of course, the absolute opposite. It is a deep respect for the office and a desire to demonstrate that it reflects the character and person of Jesus Christ, not the status of a Head of State.

JOHN 13:12-20

After he had washed their feet, had put on his robe, and had returned to the table, he said to them, 'Do you know what I have done to you? [13] You call me Teacher and Lord – and you are right, for that is what I am. [14]So if I, your Lord and Teacher, have washed your feet, you also ought to wash one another's feet. [15]For I have set you an example, that you also should do as I have done to you. [16] Very truly, I tell you, servants are not greater than their master, nor are messengers greater than the one who sent them. [17]If you know these things, you are blessed if you do them. [18]I am not speaking of all of you; I know whom I have chosen. But it is to fulfil the scripture, "The one who ate my bread has lifted his heel against me." [19]I tell you this now, before it occurs, so that when it does occur, you may believe that I am he. [20]Very truly, I tell you, whoever receives one whom I send receives me; and whoever receives me receives him who sent me.'

Jesus' disciples' reactions to having their feet washed are generally unknown. Peter speaks and is rebuked. He accepts what Jesus says and willingly receives the washing. We do not know the reaction of any of the others. However, after Jesus has returned to his place at the table, it is clear that every eye is on him, and that every heart is beating faster at the as yet incomprehensible significance of what he has done. He addresses them directly: 'You call me Teacher and Lord – and you are right, for that is what I am. So if I, your Lord and Teacher, have washed your feet, you also ought to wash one another's feet. For I have set you an example, that you also should do as I have done to you. Very truly, I tell you, servants are not greater than their master, nor are messengers greater than the one who sent them' (vv. 13-16).

There is no qualification of his authority and position. He is Teacher and Lord and the washing of feet does not change that. The significance is in what is meant by Teacher and Lord in the new era he is ushering in. In the same way as the three persons of the Trinity serve and love each other, so leadership is about service and love, not to win loyalty, respect and favour, but for its own sake, as an absolute good.

There are three aspects to the reversal. The first is one that we all recognise at once – that of humility. The Teacher and Lord serves. In our culture that feels right and proper. In its original context, this was a revolutionary leap. However, the spread of democracy and the rise of mass communication has reduced the distance between ruler and servant. We speak easily of public service. Democratically elected leaders are expected to serve the people, and their reward is limited to a salary, and to the rather questionable benefit of spending their lives surrounded by close protection, with some immunity to heavy traffic.

The second aspect is far deeper and more demanding. We are not merely to serve with humility, but also to create communities of service that model what Jesus does for his disciples. Washing feet can be done alone (most of us wash our feet by ourselves), but Jesus-style foot-washing requires company, and more than that, a community. It is to be a community of the humble servant, one that sees no point in status at the cost of others, where demeaning tasks are no longer demeaning because they are done in the name of Christ.

It is in a community so centred on Jesus that wealth or talent or anything else we receive is not ours to dispose of, but exists for others. It multiplies itself in being given, like the loaves and fishes in the story of the feeding of the 5,000. What we receive we treat as ours, yes, but the 'ours' is not personal, or even familial, or among only our natural friends. It is for all those we can find to serve. Once again, as I look into the depths of what Jesus' love means, my head spins at the endless vistas of extraordinary community and, except to the eye of faith, the infinite need and risk that it presents.

Third, just in case we feel that humility and community are not enough, we see that Jesus brings us to a new place of *how* we serve, not simply why we serve and how we lead. It is to be in love. Wealth, by being held in love for others, dethrones Mammon not through our attitudes, but through the power of Christ. The dethroning is the collateral benefit of saying that what I receive I treat not as mine, but as my opportunity to love. John 13 is agnostic about the money and power you already have. John 13 is interested in how you use that money and power – whether you put it in the service of God, and use it to wash the feet of the world; or whether you put it in the service of Mammon, and use it to insulate yourself from those whose feet smell bad.

What do you do with the power you have been given?
What do you do that seeks to insulate your own power?
Who benefits from your power?
Who else do you have the power to serve?

Jesus, having washed the disciples' feet, then returns to his seat and explains to them what he has done. He has redefined power. He has set a new standard by which his followers will be measured. No longer will they seek to compete with each other for position, but rather they will seek the welfare and benefit of those weaker than themselves. Those who seek power through wealth are living in the old age.

Now, for Christians, worldly power and status exist only for the sake of service. Washing feet breaks down any hierarchies that we might be tempted to construct between ourselves and others. It says to us that there ought to be nothing, no role or responsibility, no act of service, that falls beneath the level of our dignity. Remember Mary of Bethany, who just a chapter before this one anointed Jesus' feet and wiped them with her hair. Jesus calls this 'a beautiful thing'. This ritual of foot-washing inspires us to take on the basest roles in society and to turn them into beautiful things. This is a superpower that all Christians have – to take something that no one else wants to do, and through Christ, turn it into a beautiful thing.

Humble service is the heart of true power. And it is fundamental to the best kind of evangelism. Rodney Stark, an American sociologist, wrote a book called *The Rise of Christianity: How the Obscure, Marginal Jesus Movement Became the Dominant Religious Force in the Western World in a Few Centuries*. Stark describes himself as 'personally incapable of religious faith'. Yet he concludes in his book that one of the reasons Christianity spread so rapidly was because, when plagues swept across the ancient world (as they often did) and everyone fled the cities, it was always the Christians who stayed behind. They ministered to the sick, doing what nobody else wanted to do: touching those no one else would touch, listening to those who didn't have a voice, taking what the world called ugly and turning it into something beautiful.

We are, and have always been, in the words of Pope Francis, 'a poor church for the poor'. As I visited all the Provinces of the Anglican Communion in the first few years of my ministry as Archbishop, I saw that this characteristic of the early church – the love and compassion of the Jesus movement – is alive and well, and being demonstrated in the most extraordinary ways across the world, particularly in places of significant conflict and poverty.

John 13 is an invitation to turn the world upside down through humble acts of service. That is the Christian revolution. Jesus has given us a superpower: there is nothing in this world so ugly that it can't be turned into something beautiful with God. We must press in to those places that no one wants to go, love those who no one wants to love, abide in the places that don't smell very good, and speak to those who no one will speak to. We must wash the feet of the world.

For a long time, that is more or less what happened. The foot-washing was held to be almost as important as the communion itself. To this day, it has remained part of the liturgy for Maundy Thursday. Of course, the ritual itself gets sanitised. Human sinfulness means that being humble has to be turned into such ceremony that it does not really have much effect. Thus in many places the only people whose feet are washed are those who have been selected beforehand and who have made careful preparation, by washing their own feet, in order that the important foot washer should not be discomforted by smelly and dirty feet. That's not really what Jesus intended.

Jesus even washes the feet of Judas. He does so in full knowledge that Judas is about to betray him. In fact, for Judas, this seems to be the last straw. There is little record of what was said between them, but a few minutes later, Jesus liberates Judas to do what he has to do, and he goes out into the darkness. John simply says, 'it was night' (13:30).

The economy of humility is a complicated one by contrast to the economy of power, which is a fairly simple one.

Power and money are intimately linked, and the actions of Jesus in John 13 are as much a challenge to our concepts of money as they are to the disciples' view of power.

Money gives power. Jean Paul Getty, who was in his day the richest man in the world, pointed out: 'The meek may inherit the Earth, but not its mineral rights.' Humility is widely seen as the antithesis of power, and in fact a very good way of losing power to others.

The interaction between money and power is complex and deceptive. In the first place, money buys certain capacities. Rich countries have a wide tax base and the capacity easily to raise money for government, which enables them to spend on defence, intelligence and the exercise of soft power around the world. Rich countries can simply 'do' more, and the nature of political authority and office seeking is that what you *can* do feels like something you *should* do. Mammon tells us that if we have the wealth to achieve something, dominate somebody, lead somewhere, then we ought to do it. Jesus asks us if that involves foot-washing.

As a result, it is obvious to most neutral observers that for good or ill the world's economic system is dominated by the wealthy, who through their wealth have the power to set the terms of engagement in international trade and commerce, as well as in the exercise of hard and soft political power. These are closely associated.

For example, the economic wealth of historically Christian countries, and those whose development was influenced by them, means that the international financial system is based around the use of interest, and models of financial transactions that derive from the Protestant Christian tradition. That tradition has acquired a hegemony in world economics which means that all international analysis of the relative strength and weakness of countries' economies is driven by the underlying assumptions that the Protestant tradition brings to world markets. At their heart is acceptance, against a centuries-old trend, of interest as first a legitimate and ultimately a core aspect of trade and commerce. We are so used to this assumption that we forget how shocking it would have been to many Christians before the Reformation and would still be to adherents of many other faiths today.

It might be fine if you are in the United Kingdom, especially if you are involved in financial services. It is less good if you are a Muslim who has a principled theological objection to the use of interest. It is also less good if you come from Africa, south of the Sahara, where assumptions about wealth and poverty lead to your country being shut out of international markets to a degree that leads to an over-reliance on international aid. This in and of itself is often deeply destabilising, both politically and economically, creating distortions in the national economy that prohibit or discourage the development of the kinds of small-scale businesses that can most effectively lift the condition of the poor. Aid, which we will look at in more detail in the next chapter, is a good and necessary tool through which to support the development of particular countries, but in its application it has often been associated with personal gain by elites, and, even worse, with the exercise of power by donors over recipients. Foot-washing seeks only the good of the person being served.

It is an act of love, not an act of manipulation or mastery. It is not even an act of improvement, in seeking to transfer our values into the culture of another country or society.

Power and money are connected historically through the development of the great empires of the nineteenth century. This has been a truism for many years. Perhaps surprisingly, it was recognised by Kipling in his poem 'Recessional', written for the Diamond Jubilee of Queen Victoria. At this time, the UK held a similar position globally to the military-industrial hegemony of the USA since the fall of the Berlin Wall in 1989. Yet Kipling recognises the conditionality of power – even when, as then, it sprang from an economy that was dominant in the world – a conditionality that rested ultimately in the will of God:

> Far-called, our navies melt away;
> On dune and headland sinks the fire:
> Lo, all our pomp of yesterday
> Is one with Nineveh and Tyre!
> Judge of the Nations, spare us yet,
> Lest we forget – lest we forget!

Kipling, at the height of Britain's influence, saw the danger of hubris that came from money and power, and warned of it with striking words.

Money buys capabilities. It also buys security. Individuals are able to live in gated compounds, have chauffeur-driven cars, send their children to private schools, use private medical facilities, have space to live with spare rooms and studies and large gardens. It is possible for them to isolate themselves from the inconveniences of normal life. The use of wealth to acquire security is normal, but it risks taking us further and further away from being those who wash feet, who dethrone Mammon by subverting the power of wealth to give us a better life. The more we have, the harder we have to work at washing feet.

Barring great national catastrophes or natural disaster, money buys the rich longer lives and greater happiness, though perhaps only up to a point. A 2010 study by Princeton University's Center for Health and Well-Being[1] suggested that emotional well-being rises with income up to $75,000 (around £50,000), above which no additional well-being is observed.

PSALM 73: 1-14

Truly God is good to the upright,
　　to those who are pure in heart.
[2]But as for me, my feet had almost stumbled;
　　my steps had nearly slipped.
[3]For I was envious of the arrogant;
　　I saw the prosperity of the wicked.
[4]For they have no pain;
　　their bodies are sound and sleek.
[5]They are not in trouble as others are;
　　they are not plagued like other people.
[6]Therefore pride is their necklace;
　　violence covers them like a garment.
[7]Their eyes swell out with fatness;
　　their hearts overflow with follies.

---

⁸They scoff and speak with malice;
    loftily they threaten oppression.
⁹They set their mouths against heaven,
    and their tongues range over the earth.
¹⁰Therefore the people turn and praise them,
    and find no fault in them.
¹¹And they say, 'How can God know?
    Is there knowledge in the Most High?'
¹²Such are the wicked;
    always at ease, they increase in riches.
¹³All in vain I have kept my heart clean
    and washed my hands in innocence.
¹⁴For all day long I have been plagued,
    and am punished every morning.

Either way, it is easy to argue that the happiness is not genuine, that security is an illusion and that power fades. All that is true, yet there is something deeper. The psalmist in Psalm 73 looks at the rich and is tempted to believe that all goes well with them; then he remembers the eternal justice of God. Yet, for many much does go well, and in one sense it is good to rejoice in that. The happiness of the poor is not necessarily increased by diminishing the happiness of the rich! It is better to rejoice that we see Mammon dethroned when what is received is treated as a trust, a grace to be deployed in love.

The psalmist repeatedly makes the point that the rich live charmed lives, far from the ills that affect everyone else. For the psalmist, it causes deep doubt about the goodness of God, because he wants the rich to be seen to suffer fear and failure like everyone else. In Ecclesiastes, the preacher reflects on a world in which the failure of the rich is in their successes, in their incapacity to build durably for eternity but only for their lifetimes.

Human selfishness says that 'it will see me out' is sufficient. The modern world has moved far from the Homeric ideal that a hero's name should live forever through their descendants and through the record of their deeds. We are accustomed not merely to the fleeting fifteen minutes of fame, but to former leaders, who have dominated the press, disappearing without trace within days or months of their retirement. There is almost a sense of our jealous celebration in their new-found obscurity.

Jesus points to something deeper. In John 13, the opening verses are absolutely essential to our understanding of what happens next. They are often taken as an indication that Jesus is able to humble himself out of his own sense of profound security, arising from knowing his calling, and that he belongs to the Father. There is much more to it than that. The opening verses subvert all notions that power gives us security, and thus, because of the unshakeable link between money and power, their economic impact is profound.

As we have seen, Jesus has an unbreakable knowledge of the relationship he has with his Father. In that relationship of love, with all other powers relativised and powerless, he is able to act in self-giving love. That is our benchmark.

To what radical act of foot-washing might God be calling you?
To what simple, everyday habits of foot-washing might
God be calling you?

Jesus' act of foot-washing turns out to be a precursor of an even more radical – indeed the ultimate – act of self-giving love. The foot-washing depicts how Jesus divests himself of the robe of divinity, takes on the towel of humble humanity, and adopts the posture of a slave in washing feet. On the cross in the act of crucifixion he experiences the ultimate divesting, the complete subjection, the final self-giving. The cross is both the consummate moment of Jesus' enthronement in vulnerability for the sin of the world, and the nadir from which the arc of glory – his resurrection and ascension – begins. The foot-washing anticipates this in the way Jesus eventually sets aside the towel, reclaims the robe of his divinity, and resumes his place at the divine table.

When Peter resists Jesus washing his feet, he is unknowingly also opposing the cross: that's why Jesus is so adamant with him. Everything in Jesus' life anticipates the cross: everything in our lives is possible because of it.

5

What we give we gain

Key text *John 19:38-42*
The Burial of Jesus

It is typical for Christians to take a generally negative attitude towards money. We say, believing that we're quoting Scripture, that it is the root of all evil (the actual Scripture verse, 1 Timothy 6:10, says '*the love of money* is a root of all kinds of evil'). We criticise materialism at Christmas, chocolate at Easter and sunny holidays in August. We risk a sort of nimby-ish Puritanism. Of course, we like to have a certain amount of money ourselves, but we don't like to think that it has any significant influence on us or our attitudes. Money, we believe, is simply an unfortunate necessity of life in the world.

And our favourite cautionary tale is Ebenezer Scrooge's near miss. In the last couple of scenes of *A Christmas Carol*, Scrooge, returning from his voyages with the ghosts of Christmas Past, Present and Future, realises that he has simply been dreaming, and that he is waking in his cold, lonely house. He leans out of a window, and discovers that it is Christmas Day. Overcome with joy and relief that he hasn't missed it, and learning the lessons of his dreams, he rushes downstairs, and starts spending his money.

The family of his poor clerk are sent a goose. He goes round for a meal with his nephew, and celebrates wildly. As with all Dickens' descriptions, the writing is both over the top and immensely perceptive. Scrooge is seen as gaining from what he gives. His life as a miser has been one of broken relationships, lost loves, oppressed employees, loneliness and poverty in almost every way. His life as a generous man makes him infinitely richer. It is a life lived in community with restored relationships, and rejoicing in generosity. What Scrooge gives away turns out still to be small fare when compared to what he gains in return. What we give we gain.

What we gain when we give comes in many forms. First of all, when we give, we recognise, both implicitly and explicitly, that life is not a process of exchange and equivalence, but of abundance and generosity. This contrast comes from the writings of Paul Ricoeur,[1] specifically comparing the divine and human economies. Exchange and equivalence is a zero-sum approach, the notion that what I give I lose to your gain. It implies a closed system. Abundance and generosity implies an open system, one in which the creative power of God is ever active, so what we give we gain. Mammon wants us to believe that the books always have to balance out in the end – that whatever you have is what I can't have and vice versa. Financial markets, commodity markets, even the national accounts are drawn up on this basis, thanks to a system of double-entry bookkeeping devised in the medieval period by a Franciscan monk. When the oil price drops, within the closed system of the global economy, consumers gain at the cost of producers. When one country's exchange rate depreciates, or falls in value, then the goods of that country become cheaper abroad, but the goods of its competitors become relatively more expensive. In the last few years, that has led to countries seeking to force their currencies into competitive devaluations in order to achieve better exports. And in our globalised world economy, we have increasingly seen the problems of one economy, whether of inflation or unemployment or under-investment, exported around the world, with clear negative effects.

Mammon is good at arithmetic, and balancing the books, but very bad at divine economics. Mammon's economy is based on the principle of 'beggar your neighbour'. But in divine economics, where there is abundance and generosity, there is no zero-sum approach. Instead, we see an economy that facilitates mutual flourishing and the common good. Pope Benedict XVI describes this at the very end of his 2009 encyclical *Caritas in Veritate*, where he calls for economics to include the principle of gratuity, of giving without the expectation of anything in return, which can be interpreted as 'grace in action'.

Of course, many people admire abundance and generosity in others and might wish to do the same, but lack the abundance with which to be generous. We can only give that which we already have. I will return to that in a moment, but for those who do have any Scrooge-like resources, giving away gains everything. In other words, where our own circumstances give us the capacity to be generous, where we are the receivers of abundance, the reformed Scrooge should be our model. Abundance exists to be given, freely and openly.

In recent years, a number of high-profile economists have convincingly demonstrated that the social instability which arises from increasing inequality also increases fear, and the kind of instability that erodes any quality-of-life gains achieved by the rich. Thomas Piketty's *Capital in the Twenty-First Century* is perhaps the best-known offering in this genre. As mentioned earlier, in the 1980s, there was a growing belief in trickle-down theory, the idea that wealth among the rich would percolate down to the rest of society. By 2008, the falsity of this approach could clearly be seen, and it forms an important part of Piketty's writing. Inequality and instability in society are linked, thus once again Mammon tricks us.

In the chapters of this book, we have considered those episodes from Jesus' life that immediately preceded his crucifixion. We have been walking with Jesus towards the cross. In this chapter, we will consider what happens in the immediate aftermath of Jesus' death; specifically by looking at the actions of two minor characters: Joseph of Arimathea and Nicodemus. The actions of these men are highly significant, but are often overshadowed by the immensity of the cross itself.

JOHN 19:38-42

After these things, Joseph of Arimathea, who was a disciple of Jesus, though a secret one because of his fear of the Jews, asked Pilate to let him take away the body of Jesus. Pilate gave him permission; so he came and removed his body. [39]Nicodemus, who had at first come to Jesus by night, also came, bringing a mixture of myrrh and aloes, weighing about a hundred pounds. [40]They took the body of Jesus and wrapped it with the spices in linen cloths, according to the burial custom of the Jews. [41]Now there was a garden in the place where he was crucified, and in the garden there was a new tomb in which no one had ever been laid. [42]And so, because it was the Jewish day of Preparation, and the tomb was nearby, they laid Jesus there.

The response of Joseph of Arimathea and Nicodemus to the death of Jesus was simple: they organised and presided over his burial. The manner in which they did so dethroned Mammon. But first, let us again try to put ourselves in their Holy Week shoes.

The tomb is described in all four Gospels as new, one in which nobody had previously been laid. The body is embalmed with a huge quantity of spices – an excessive amount, indicating the love and generosity of Joseph of Arimathea and those with him. The whole process is completed in a rush, because the Sabbath is fast approaching. As soon as it has been completed, the tomb is sealed (and, in Matthew's Gospel, a guard is put on it to prevent the body being stolen) and those of the disciples who have played any part and who have not already abandoned Jesus then disperse.

The story exists principally to emphasise the reality of the death and burial of Jesus. It is clear from the Gospel accounts that rumours circulated that either he had not died, or that his body had been stolen by the disciples. All four Gospel writers go to great lengths to demonstrate that neither of these stories is remotely credible.

At the time of Jesus' death, the disciples' view of the world would have been bleak in the extreme. They had spent the

previous week preparing for Jesus' victory. All the momen-
tum was behind this leader who gathered his followers and
marched on the capital city. Instead of a victory, their leader
endured an ignominious, unjust and illegal trial held under
the cover of night. He had been wrongfully convicted and
executed. Not only that, but Joseph and Nicodemus witnessed
the flight of Jesus' main supporters in his greatest hour of
need. The crowds that had gathered, less than a week before,
waving palms and laying down their cloaks to usher in their
new king, had gathered again around Jesus. Now, however,
they were yelling 'Crucify him', and then they dispersed.
Those who expected to find themselves in power, now found
themselves on the outside once again.

God appeared to have shut up shop and gone home. There
was no intervention, apart from the deep darkness that fell
at around the time of the execution, and an earthquake. The
disciples may have heard rumours of unexplained damage to
the curtain of the temple that covered the Holy of Holies.
Regardless of that, there was no indication that they had any
hope of seeing Jesus again, and no indication that there was
any force or power left in the Jesus movement. Jesus was,
literally, dead weight. To do anything for him at this time
can only be seen as gratuitous generosity, springing from the
abundance which Joseph of Arimathea had experienced in
knowing Jesus.

Yet that is exactly what Joseph and Nicodemus do. When
everyone else has abandoned Jesus, in the darkest hour of
them all, they act with extraordinary generosity. Joseph of
Arimathea acquires permission from Pilate to take Jesus down
from the cross and to have him buried in his own tomb – a

tomb that, again, all four Gospels point out has never before been used. Nicodemus assists Joseph in the burial by bringing a large quantity of spices with which to anoint Jesus' body. Such an act was deeply irrational.

Do you remember a time when you received an absurdly generous gift? How did you respond?
Did that gift have an effect on gifts you gave in the future?
If so, how?

At this point, let me introduce two characters whom we know, but perhaps not by these names. The first is *homo economicus*. The second is his sibling, *homo financiarius*. Economicus is to Financiarius as Sherlock Holmes is to his brother Mycroft. Economicus is the better known, but Financiarius wields the greater influence. Economicus is the invention of modern economics. Let us call them Cony and Fin for short.

Cony is a person who makes decisions on the basis of a carefully thought-through rational impetus to maximise their own personal advantage. When everyone behaves like that, the economy should work very well indeed. Thus, Cony is only generous when that will do some direct or indirect good. For instance, giving might be valued because it generates fame or attracts friends or clients. So secret giving would be of no value, unless there was some inner satisfaction from having done it. Cony is addicted to facts and reasons, to logic and calculation. Virtue is an irrelevance; consequentialism rules in all decisions. He or she acts because, after careful thought, he/she has foreseen the outcome, or range of outcomes. Based on a risk-weighted calculation of probable results, he/she acts to their own advantage. *If* we believed in Cony, and *if* markets all behaved rationally, and *if* there were no bits of metaphorical grit in the global economic system which make it work less than perfectly and *if* … Well, you get the picture. One might as well say that if the world were flat the sun would rise at the same time everywhere. And the answer is always 'but it isn't'. So Cony lives in an imaginary world, but Mammon has somehow managed to convince the economies of the world that it is real, and thus to make plans and operate on a basis that is false.

Financiarius is the younger sibling who came to maturity after the Big Bang in 1986. Fin is not interested in the actual transfer of goods and services – what is often called the 'real' economy – but operates in the misty and often mythical world of options and futures, of derivative financial instruments, and mathematical calculations which somehow enable him or her to become very wealthy indeed, without ever creating or touching anything real. It is Fin's influence that means that the proportion of financial transactions to real economic transactions has increased by a factor of fifty in this time, according to some estimates. As one economist notes, this means that 'for every dollar of added value that is created today, twenty-five dollars are traded on financial markets, compared with just fifty cents thirty-five years ago'.[2]

To put that simply, in 1980, for every pound you spent on buying or selling something, whether goods or services, financial transactions in the economy were worth about £2.70. By 2010, they were worth about £14.00. That extra volume of financial transactions did not represent an increase in the wealth of the country in any systematic way, but was mostly confined to transactions between financial companies, banks and other members of the financial services industry. Mostly it was for their own profit and loss account, and often built on staggeringly complex structures of mathematical calculation about the relationship between different commodities, or the possible future development of the value of currencies or commodities. The resulting volume of financial transactions is an inverted pyramid, in which those who work in the international financial and commodity markets are balanced ever more precariously on what is happening in the real economy underneath.

Trading in the market is something that relies very much on exchange and equivalence. Cony and Fin feel quite comfortable there, or would do, if Cony was not a myth and Fin a deception.

Cony is a myth because most of us do not make decisions on transactions for entirely rational purposes. Emotion also plays a part. We buy a takeaway because we are tired, and we fancy sitting down in front of the telly with a beer. We buy a different car, despite meticulous research, because we like the sales assistant. We give presents to each other not because it is our turn, but because we love each other.

And so on, and so on. Cony does not exist. Fin is even worse, because Fin claims to be of value, while adding no value except in book terms and to a tiny number of rich people. Is this the jaundiced meanderings of a priest who wishes he was back in the financial markets making more money? In fact, this echoes the assessment of the Chairman of the Financial

Services Authority in 2009, who described much of the activity of the financial market as being 'socially useless'; the former Chair of the British Bankers Association said that some financial products are 'of no real use to humanity'.

Cony and Fin are Mammon in another guise. They both represent an enthroned view of quantitative measurement, and a dismissal of those who have little economic contribution to make. They tell us that they are the truth and that they rule every aspect of human existence. In fact, deep inside, most of us – including the majority of those who work in the markets – know that Cony and Fin, like Mammon, are liars. They are convenient ways of rationalising the irrational behaviour of vast crowds of people, of seeking to put order on to chaos. As we will see, Joseph of Arimathea and Nicodemus put order in place through gratuity – love expressed without expectation of return. The lies of Mammon that dictate the terms of our economy must be replaced with the abundance and gratuity of Jesus Christ, which Joseph and Nicodemus imitate.

Joseph of Arimathea is related neither to Cony nor to Fin. Of all the economically valueless things, a dead body must come top of the list. In many religions, it brings ritual impurity. It is likely to carry disease. It will never again demonstrate affection. It will certainly never add productive value to the economy. You might even say that Jesus' body was particularly value-less. Jesus was an unmarried, poor, itinerant rabbi. He had no inheritance to pass on. Yes, he had a kind of celebrity status; yes, people had marched behind him into Jerusalem, but the revolution had come up short. It had failed. Jesus was defeated, and those who expected deliverance ended up with embarrassment. Few see any worth in caring for the dead; fewer still for embarrassing celebrity failures like Jesus. Even those closest to him were nowhere to be found when his body was lowered from the cross.

All of us who have been bereaved at one point or another know that extraordinary sense of finality that comes with death. Joseph of Arimathea does something that is irrational, generous and loving to Jesus, with no conceivable advantage to himself at all. In fact, it will be of considerable disadvantage, because he has used up the newness of the tomb with someone who is not a family member. Nicodemus, joining him, is also doing something that is of no value; in fact, you might say it is of immensely negative value. For a Pharisee, being in contact with a dead body made one unclean, which would be bad enough at any time of the year. The fact that he would be unclean for the Passover Sabbath made this act an unforgivable disaster. Nicodemus chose to deny himself a part in the central festival of the Jewish year for the sake of Jesus – even after Jesus had been crucified, even after all hope was lost. Moreover, by associating with the dead Jesus, who had been betrayed by the leaders of the Jewish people, Nicodemus was condemning himself to further social exclusion. In Joseph and Nicodemus, Jesus had won two public disciples at a point when it was too late for them to gain any measurable advantage from it at all.

From Cony's point of view, as we have seen, these risky, polluting and costly gestures of Joseph and Nicodemus were of little or no value. Yet in God's extraordinary economy, it was of immense value, because their gifts reflect the very nature of God, who gives by grace without expecting a return,

just as in the parable of the pearl of great price (Matthew
13:45-6). That is the very definition of grace: love given without the expectation of return. Joseph and Nicodemus act in
accordance with a radically different economy. They have
experienced Jesus, so Mammon has been dethroned in their
imaginations. They see the world through different eyes, when
spending extraordinary amounts of money on something
that is of no economic significance can be of extraordinary
spiritual significance. What they gave materially was repaid
spiritually tenfold.

With this picture in our minds – of two depressed and
despairing disciples doing something out of mere love
and goodwill, without any hope of it making any difference to
them or anyone else – let us look at how we too can experience that what we give, we gain.

In the story of the burial of Jesus, money becomes a way of
ascribing eternal value through the use of temporary value.
There is a time shift that is very dramatic. Joseph's money could
not have lasted forever. If he did not spend it, his descendants
certainly would. Through what he does, he expresses value
in a way that has become eternal, and the temporary value of
money has been transformed into something that lasts to this
day. He demonstrates that what he owns is not for his benefit but for the common good, in solidarity with others, in
his own time and for generations to come. The possession of
money is a God-given right to identify with people, to show
solidarity, to transform the world for the better.

Here is an example. The giving of international aid is very
much a twentieth century concept. During the period before
the Second World War, in the time of global empires, some

imperial rulers felt it necessary to provide aid, perhaps in response to a natural disaster, but even then the giving of aid was intermittent and inefficient. In the nineteenth century, natural disasters such as famine or plague were seen as somehow inevitable, and there was no great sense that they should be resisted. The appalling Irish potato famines of the mid-1840s did not attract any great response from the British Government, until the suffering became so acute, and the newspaper reports so effective, that there seemed no alternative to providing at least some moderate support. Even so, the impact on the Irish population was vast and permanent. It is one of the greatest scandals of the British Imperial Age.

Where a country was not under imperial rule – such as much of China in the nineteenth century – famine and suffering led to no action at all. Following the Second World War, the pattern was broken in many ways by the Marshall Plan. Europe after 1945 was in a state of total collapse, with nearly 20 million people on the move as refugees. This happened to coincide with two or three very severe winters. The suffering of people whose houses had been bombed and whose economies had collapsed as a result of war was beyond description.

The response by the USA was overwhelmingly generous and immensely effective. It provided the relaunch of the European economies and the Golden Era, which lasted until 1973 and the first oil crisis. During that time inflation remained relatively low, growth was constant and significant, and, year by year, people grew richer. The USA transferred enormous sums of money, hundreds of billions of dollars in today's terms, in aid and support for both the vanquished and the victors on the continent of Europe. It was especially notable that they gave such large sums to Germany, which until a few months earlier they had been fighting with every last resource at their disposal.

The Marshall Plan has become proverbial as something that is overwhelmingly generous, and that springs out of deep humanitarian and Christian impulses, not only economic ones. The more cynical among the economists argue that it was in America's self-interest to make such donations. But the writings of the time show that, while there was some truth in this, in general the impulse was deeply Christian and compassionate. Marshall Aid, together with the founding of the International Bank for Reconstruction and Development (now the World Bank), and the International Monetary Fund, arose out of the fertile imagination of John Maynard Keynes in the great conference to settle the post-war economic system at Bretton Woods in the USA. That conference and international agreement established an example which was and continues to be followed both systematically and internationally.

The World Bank was founded with the obligation to finance affordable loans to countries in need of reconstruction and development. Since then, its mandate has extended far wider and, although there are often complaints about its bureaucracy and its attitudes, its history is in general a glorious one.

Bit by bit, equivalent organisations were established around the world, on most continents. In addition, countries began to set aside money for international development. For many years, this had rather mixed motives – to enable international development, but also to help the donor country's own trade system. Thus, for example, UK aid was usually tied to the buying of UK goods, until 1997 when the newly formed

Department for International Development (DFID) was spun out of the Foreign and Commonwealth Office. In 2013, the UK became one of the very few countries to reach the United Nations target of 0.7 per cent of our national income being given in aid – a target that had been agreed 40 years earlier. The astonishing thing was that this target was reached at a time of the utmost financial austerity, following the Great Recession, and was set and delivered despite it having no popular appeal. In fact, ever since its creation, DFID has been the object of remorseless attack by much of the press and many in parliament.

The combination of this fixed percentage of Gross National Income (GNI), and a growing economy, means that the aid budget has grown significantly, and will continue to do so while the economy grows. On top of that, the disconnection since 1997 between aid and the compulsory purchase of British exports has meant that DFID has become one of the world leaders in development, with very significant results in many of its projects. According to official figures, between 2011 and 2015, over 43 million children have been immunised against preventable diseases with DFID funding and support, almost 30 million infants and their mothers supported through its nutrition programmes and 11 million children supported in education. The sophistication of DFID is exceptional, a world leader that has found an effective way to give that is both generous and strategic.

What we give we gain. This rather lengthy section on our international aid budget, and the history of international giving since 1945, is to demonstrate the huge shift that has occurred in the way that wealthy countries look at questions of development, and above all questions of aid. This is not to deny that aid has been badly used and misspent. Often it has been, serving as a form of trade subsidy, or a way of generating soft power, or even appeasing colonial guilt, as a case of 'if we give we can't be that bad'. To this day, large countries in sub-Saharan Africa rely on aid for a dangerous percentage of their national income. It is very easy to see that it has often been diverted into corruption, and there are obvious targets in attacking its misuse. It is also notoriously hard to measure the effectiveness of 'development spend', which makes DFID an easy political target.

Yet what the critics ignore, and what our friend Cony fails to understand, is the biblical view that the giving of help, or the forgiving of debts, is of far greater importance for the giver than for the recipient. In the spiritual economy, whether at a national or a personal level, giving is a good thing which brings the blessing of God. But how does this work? How is it that giving without expectation of return actually results in some return in God's economy?

Giving builds links with people whom we may not know and can never reach or meet in any other way. Relationship is hugely important in giving, but it is not indispensable. We can in fact start relationships simply through our own generosity.

At a national scale, a very good example is found in Sierra Leone. In the late 1990s, a civil war, linked in some degree to the presence of diamond mines in the country, led to a rebel group exercising the most extraordinary cruelty as they sought to take over the country. They made a habit of cutting off the arms of those they'd captured, using expressions like 'long sleeves' (the arm cut off below the elbow) and 'short sleeves' (the arm cut off above the elbow). Even the use of African Union troops to try and hold them was only partially successful. A small British force was dispatched, initially to evacuate British citizens from the capital, Freetown, before it fell to the rebels. When they found that, faced with disciplined troops, the rebel forces dispersed in disarray, the decision was made to push forward and overwhelm the enemy forces. They succeeded, and Sierra Leone fairly rapidly achieved a state of relative stability, and in fact managed to create a court which was effective in trying crimes against humanity committed by the rebel forces.

For those in Sierra Leone (I visited a couple of years later), the British were the great heroes. The UK had given, through the commitment of forces, and then through considerable aid and development assistance, to a country in which we had no great strategic interest, but out of a sense of compassion and generosity. The British abolitionists of the late eighteenth and early nineteenth centuries – including William Wilberforce – were instrumental in the development of Freetown and Sierra Leone as a home for freed slaves. Our link went back a long way, and goes to the heart of our values and sensibilities.

In 2014, Ebola broke out in Sierra Leone. With a dispatch of troops to build field hospitals and medical facilities, and improve communications, and also with significant humanitarian aid, the United Kingdom was one of the largest single responders to the Ebola crisis in Sierra Leone and beyond. It took a while to get the effort against Ebola up to the level it should have been, yet that was not what was noticed by the local people. When I went there in December 2014, for a very brief visit, the comment everywhere was that no one except the British had come to their aid, and we'd done it twice. The average UK citizen might not realise it, but generosity, giving away, had gained us relationships and gratitude in God's economy that link us in a profound way to a country of which most people have heard very little and few have ever visited.

Money is one part of the God-given economy of abundance which enables us to show solidarity and to build relationships. It brings us closer to people far away. One of the most striking philanthropists in the world today is Bill Gates, the founder of Microsoft. He stepped down from Microsoft a few years ago, in order to run the Bill & Melinda Gates Foundation, which is managed with the same rigour and focus that he brought to Microsoft when he was in charge.

He remains one of the richest men on earth, but the vast bulk of his wealth is now dedicated to the effort to eliminate various critical diseases that cause so much premature death in large parts of the world. The money is dispersed very carefully, and with immense thoughtfulness and strategic purpose. All that is good, and in one sense brings him the reward of being widely known and admired.

Yet there is something far more important. Both he and his wife, Melinda, with their children, travel constantly to places where they will be profoundly uncomfortable, in order to see what is happening, and to build better relationships with those they meet.

Strictly speaking, what they do personally is entirely unnecessary. The work would probably go forward pretty much as well if they just relied on written reports, and dispatched highly trained experts to see where things were going well and where they were going badly. Yet, entirely consciously, they are using their wealth to create links and relationships, with a great aim in mind, but with the effect along the way of enabling value to be given to those to whom they give money.

In God's economy, the value of the person is not set by the money we give them, or the value of a nation by the aid it receives. The value is set by the very fact that we give, especially when we give sacrificially. The value of the aid, especially when it is difficult to spare, creates links that are far deeper than what the money itself buys.

What gifts have you given that were particularly meaningful for you to give? Why?

Joseph of Arimathea and Nicodemus, by their contribution of wealth and effort, made it clear that Jesus was of a value to them which surpassed social status, and indeed life itself. A corpse is not an asset, yet the bodies of those whom we love are commonly treated with dignity wherever this is possible. The failure to treat the dead with dignity is seen as a sign of an absolute breakdown in order, or of a deep failure of humanity. Many will remember seeing a BBC reporter in New Orleans after Hurricane Katrina, losing his temper with a police officer who was standing negligently near a body which had been lying on an overpass above the water for some days. The reporter's shock was that in a country as prosperous as the USA, the basic dignity that should be ascribed to the dead had been neglected. God's economy had broken down under the impact of selfishness and fear.

What does that mean for us as individuals? There are some very practical implications.

The first implication is that we need to train ourselves to see the world in terms of abundance and generosity, rather than being conformed by Cony and Fin to ideas of equivalence and exchange. Such a discipline swims against the stream of the way the economy is assumed to work. The habit of weekly or monthly giving, starting with the Church to enable it to carry out its vision, and going beyond to other things that are in our hearts as we pray and reflect about them, is a very good way of setting our budget. Even if it is a very small amount, giving should be at the top of the list of what we do, and our income should be considered net of what we give before we decide what we spend. How different could our world look if we thought of giving as an obligation, like our taxes, rather than a luxury extra?

What opportunities are there in your own budget to put more emphasis on giving?

The way the Church sets budgets is as important as the way it writes its theology, as a budget is applied theology expressed in numbers. The Church of England is seeking to reshape its budget to spend more on ministry with the poor, and on mission. Resources may be limited, but the way they are deployed shows our vision of the God who gives them to us. A friend of mine who was the parish priest in an area of considerable poverty remembered a churchwarden saying, in response to the suggestion that the church should give away a small proportion of its income, 'What do you think we are, vicar: a charity?'

One of the more surreal parts of my job is the accommodation that comes with it: Lambeth Palace. There has been an almost continual Christian presence on the site of the Palace since the thirteenth century, serving as the home to my predecessors. Of course, the nature of the role of Archbishop of Canterbury has evolved since then, and today some question whether such palatial accommodation is really appropriate. In many ways, I share this unease. In the spirit of the previous chapter, it is important to resist the temptation to treat Lambeth Palace as anything other than an extraordinary (temporary) gift, and therefore to take seriously my responsibility to steward it as an example of God's abundance and generosity. We are always seeking to make it a more open and hospitable place that can be a blessing for all who use it.

The church in Philippi is held up by Paul in his second letter to the Corinthians as a model for giving (see 2 Corinthians 8:1-7), acting out of poverty but in love for the church in Jerusalem. They are contrasted with Corinth, which is proving slow in making its own contribution, despite its wealth. Theologically, Paul locates the abundance of God in Jesus Christ as a lavish gift that opened salvation to the world. Abundance and grace lived out is thus a measure of our discipleship, both as individuals and as churches. It is rooted in the very nature of God. It does not seek to accumulate but, like Joseph of Arimathea and Nicodemus, spends generously and at personal risk, because it is rooted in the love of God in Christ.

The second implication of God's economy for us as individuals is to recognise that there is a political aspect to our actions. As we are part of a nation that is funding international aid through the tax system, that needs to be a subject of our prayers, and our praise. Praise to God for what has happened, and praise to governments for what they have been disciplined enough to persist in, despite all the political disincentives. Aid is not popular, not least because Mammon is so strong. There are always great needs in the donor country that could be met through diverting the aid budget. We are called to be good stewards of our money, and part of that is about discerning how we give and ensuring that we give with wisdom. But as I have said in this chapter, the true impact of giving is not seen if we only consider it through the eyes of Cony and Fin.

How might we best pray for those in positions of political leadership who are responsible for our local, national and international finances?

The third and final implication I want to identify is that we should see money as an instrument that enables us to build relationships of abundance and grace. Do not be ashamed of spending on each other, on those we love, on those we don't know and on those who – according to Cony and Fin – have no value to us; but, in doing so, seek to build a relationship that is enabled by the use of money.

Try to list those people whom you see regularly in the course
of your daily or weekly life, and whose names you know.
Which of those relationships are founded on exchange and
equivalence? Which are built on abundance and grace?

Are there relationships in your own life that would benefit from
being built on abundance and grace, rather than
exchange and equivalence?
What might be the first step in facilitating the
transformation of those relationships?

Abundance and grace call us to be generous and trusting, in a way that builds links and relationships. Trust in the economy of God leads us to seek to give because to do so is to gain. The gain may be less tangible than our money was, and the revolution in our thinking that is required is enormous. We start with small steps, and will find that Mammon first shudders, then falls from the throne. No longer will his reign be supported by our own wrongful attitudes and the structures that dominate how we measure value and importance in our world.

We know that the tomb is not the end of the story. For Jesus, his death was not a zero-sum game. Because of the grace and abundance of God, Jesus Christ rose again and ascended to the throne. When Mammon is dethroned, we are not faced with an empty throne, but one from which Christ's mastery brings order, justice and joy. In the final chapter, we consider the implications of this for our relationship with money.

In what way might God be calling you to be generous this Lent?

6

What we master brings us joy

Key texts *Revelation 3:14-22 The Message to Laodicea*
and *Revelation 18 The Fall of Babylon*

We have a tendency to think about money as people in the prohibition era thought about alcohol. Although there is nothing specifically in the Bible that justifies its banning, we feel that its effects are so often bad that there must be something inherently wrong with it. It should probably be outlawed altogether, or, if we can't do that, we should at the very least strongly discourage its use, lest we become this evil force's next victim. While this conviction applied to money may very well be the product of good intentions, it is nonetheless a very dangerous one. The Bible clearly does not disapprove of money – quite the reverse, in fact. From God's blessing on Abraham's wealth, through to the generosity of the early apostles, we can clearly see a scripturally positive view of money.

Yet, when we look around the world at how it is used or, rather, how it uses those who think they own it, we see that the harmful effects are frequent, not only for the wealthy, or in unequal societies, but also for a huge proportion of people who deal with money. For almost everyone it becomes a worry, or a problem, or a diversion from deeper matters.

Both the Old and New Testaments have plenty of passages that are very fierce about money. We have already looked at some of these, and at the underlying assumptions about how value is measured in the world. We have looked at how we measure progress and growth and how, in all these cases, a reliance on money or economics as the final arbiter of value leads to a deep deception. Yet because we can measure it, because we can see it, because we think we understand it, we believe that we are in charge; or even if we are not in charge, we believe that there is no alternative to relying on money as the means whereby everything is measured and valued.

We may think it is unpleasant to have Mammon on the throne, but, at the same time, we have a nasty suspicion that this false god is pretty firmly stuck to the seat, and that the alternatives are too dreadful to contemplate. History is full of those who have tried to contemplate the alternatives, and have indeed found them terrible. George Orwell, in his book *Animal Farm*, put together a fable that vividly sets out the fallacy of a humanly achieved equal society. In the story, the animals on a farm with a cruel owner overthrow his rule, and set up a cooperative in which all are equal. But as time goes on, the pigs develop more and more skills in running the farm, and award themselves, through manipulation and cruelty, greater and greater rights. The story ends with the situation as bad as, or even worse, than it was at the beginning. All animals are equal, yes. But some are more equal than others.

Other examples abound through history.[1] All of them demonstrate that efforts to impose equality always fail. Orwell's chilling fable drew on his experience of witnessing similar failure in the Spanish Civil War. It does not seem to be natural for people to accept commonality of goods, and its imposition invariably leads to terror imposed by those seeking it and evasion by those suffering it. Money and power go together, as we have seen, and the combination is toxic for human beings whose nature tends towards the misuse of both.

In the twentieth century, the history of communism, whether in the Soviet Union and Eastern Europe, or in China, Cambodia, Vietnam and North Korea, was one of the most unspeakable cruelty. Efforts to chase money and its mastery out of the system simply resulted in the domination of the system by a group of people who became richer and richer, creating inequalities that surpassed those they sought to replace.

The greatest expansion of riches, and reduction in poverty, famine and general want, has been under the market economies of the post-Second World War era. As China recovered from the Cultural Revolution (1966–76) and opened parts of its economy, especially agriculture, to market forces, famine became a thing of the past for many millions, and almost half a billion people were lifted out of poverty. Vietnam and Cambodia are going through a similar process.

When we see inequality, and read the condemnation of avarice and voracious enrichment that runs throughout the Bible, do we therefore conclude that this is mere Utopianism, not to be taken too seriously? Do we shrug and accept that Mammon must remain on the throne, even if given a little shake from time to time, because his means of managing human greed in a way that benefits at least a significant proportion of the population are better than the Gospel of Jesus Christ? Do we conclude that all attempts to dethrone Mammon have to be kept to the individual level? Will any more widespread dethroning result in the grim Puritanism that we associate with the mid-seventeenth century or the savage cruelties of the twentieth century?

The Christian answer to all those questions is 'don't give up'. There is no doubt that centralised control of an economy is foolish. It is simply too complex a system to be controllable. The millions of transactions that make for reasonable pricing, adequate supply and equitable distribution cannot be controlled by top-down means. Adam Smith recognised this in the seventeenth century and referred to 'the invisible hand', which describes the logic of individual human behaviour within an economic system. Democratic capitalism, a twentieth century development with a number of variants and models, is a force with huge potential for good, a potential that has been more visible and demonstrable than any of the alternatives that have yet been invented.

That does not mean that Mammon should rule, because democratic capitalism also has a huge potential for injustice. Presidential elections in the United States, not least the 2016 election, have been much influenced by capitalists with great wealth, dedicated to what has been described by Jane Mayer as 'the tax deductible sponsorship of libertarianism in America'. [2] Mayer sums up the process as 'weaponising philanthropy'. [3] In a previous chapter, we looked at the nature of *homo economicus* and *homo financiarius* (Cony and Fin) and recognised that they are myths. Simple rationality doesn't govern our economic decision making, and finance subdues even economics in its desperate attempt to increase wealth, ever more speedily for an ever-smaller number of people, who then manipulate power to maintain their wealth. Mammon is triumphant.

When Mammon is dethroned, and Christ takes its place, we do not have cruelty, but love and grace. We do not have short-age, but abundance and human flourishing. We do not have deception, but we have truth. To say these things is to advo-cate money being mastered and Mammon being dethroned in both the hearts of the individual and the systems of society. In this chapter, we will look at two passages from the book of Revelation, both of which describe the deception and its cure, and offer hope and joy.

REVELATION 3:14-22

'And to the angel of the church in Laodicea write: The words of the Amen, the faithful and true witness, the origin of God's creation:

[15]'I know your works; you are neither cold nor hot. I wish that you were either cold or hot. [16]So, because you are luke-warm, and neither cold nor hot, I am about to spit you out of my mouth. [17]For you say, "I am rich, I have prospered, and I need nothing." You do not realise that you are wretched, pitiable, poor, blind, and naked. [18]Therefore I counsel you to buy from me gold refined by fire so that you may be rich; and white robes to clothe you and to keep the shame of your nakedness from being seen; and salve to anoint your eyes so that you may see. [19]I reprove and discipline those whom I love. Be earnest, therefore, and repent. [20] Listen! I

am standing at the door, knocking; if you hear my voice and open the door, I will come in to you and eat with you, and you with me. ²¹To the one who conquers I will give a place with me on my throne, just as I myself conquered and sat down with my Father on his throne. ²²Let anyone who has an ear listen to what the Spirit is saying to the churches.'

In Revelation 3:14-22, the writer of Revelation (called John, and often thought to be the Apostle John himself, or one of his disciples) is relaying the words of the glorified Christ, revealed to him in a vision while on the Isle of Patmos. Chapters 2 and 3 of Revelation consist of letters, each following a simi-lar form, addressed to seven churches across what is now southwest Turkey. Seven is a significant number, indicating completeness, so these are letters to the whole Church, pick-ing up faults and strengths that apply in one way or another to all churches at some point in every part of the world. Yet, at the same time, they address the contemporary situation of each of the seven.

There is much discussion about the nature of the meaning of some of the words in the book of Revelation.⁴ Each letter is addressed to the angel of the church in that place. This is taken to mean either a guardian angel for that church, or the local bishop. Each letter begins with a reference back to John's vision in Revelation 1, and to the speaker, the glorified Christ. The letter in Revelation 3:14-22 is to the church in Laodicea, and begins by saying that it comes from 'the Amen, the faith-ful and true witness, the origin of God's creation' (3:14). John does not waste a single word in the book of Revelation.

Everything is connected, although the forcefulness of the imagery and the vividness of the colour used often lead us to assume that it is some kind of random series of images and visions, rather than a carefully collated and thoughtfully presented whole. John reminds the Laodiceans that the words of the letter come from the 'Amen' (the final word), the faithful and true witness, the origin of God's creation. This is to tell them that what they are about to hear is definitive, is true, and speaks to the reality of everything. It is not a letter for a passing moment, but something that addresses what it is to be human, and what it is to live in God's creation.

Each letter then continues with the phrase, 'I know your works', which is a way of communicating that each of these churches is truly and utterly exposed before God. There is no hiding. God knows who they truly are – their strengths and weaknesses, their triumphs and their faults. The problem for Laodicea is that they have deceived themselves about the nature of their wealth and quality of life. In other words, Mammon is on the throne and they think it is Christ.

Are there parts of your life where you have mistaken Mammon
for Jesus?
What effect did it have?

Let me explain more fully. Laodicea was near Colossae, and also near Hierapolis. It was on a crossroads for two major trade routes, and in consequence was a great centre for exchange of goods, which were 'transhipped' rather than simply sold into Laodicea itself. Today's equivalent would be a port like

Rotterdam, where well over half the containers go in on one
ship and out on another, or on another form of transport.

As a result, like many trading cities (London or Liverpool
would be two other great examples), it developed a strong
commercial life. There was a significant banking sector (Fin's
ancestors felt very at home in Laodicea), and it also had some
of its own products, especially a very luxuriant black wool,
and a very well-known form of eye-salve. When I was growing
up, when we got sore eyes in the summer from sand blowing
on the beach, we were always given Optrex. I am sure it was
meant to be very effective, but it never seemed to do the
childish me much good! By contrast, I imagine that those who
put on some Laodicean eye-salve (Laodex?) felt much better.
Theirs was then a prosperous city, with some useful products,
much finance and certain needs.

One unusual feature of Laodicean life was that it had no
water supply of its own. Nearby, Hierapolis had hot springs,
which were known for their healing quality. Colossae had cold
springs, well known as refreshing. But the waters merged,
and by the time they got to Laodicea, they had become salty
and tepid.

This explains the frequently misunderstood verse from
Revelation 3:16: 'Because you are lukewarm, and neither
cold nor hot, I am about to spit you out of my mouth.' This
verse is often explained as suggesting that Jesus would prefer
people to have no spiritual life at all rather than a tepid one
(although obviously he would prefer a hot spiritual life). Such
an explanation is patently absurd. He wants the Church to be
either healing or refreshing – and preferably both – but not a
nauseous mixture that is neither one thing nor the other.

No church ever escapes being infected by the spirit of the age. This was certainly true of Laodicea. Jesus says to the Laodiceans, 'For you say, "I am rich, I have prospered and I need nothing." You do not realise that you are wretched, pitiable, poor, blind and naked.' These words are ferocious. They profoundly challenge the Laodicean Christians' view of themselves. Their wealth is an illusion. The word for 'poor' could be translated as destitute. Their spiritual poverty is not likened to the poverty of being a little short of the readies, but to the deeper poverty of rough sleeping, of not having any clothes, of sickness and total despair. This complacent church is actually rolling around in the gutter with nothing on. In consequence, it is in great danger of death.

The glorified Christ then gives advice (which echoes Isaiah 55) to these resourceless and deceived people, that they should 'buy' from him 'gold refined by fire so that you may be rich' (v. 18) and all the other things they need to be clothed, and to have their eyes healed so that they may see properly. It is, of course, a ridiculous piece of advice. How can someone who is destitute buy gold? The answer is that we buy from Christ with the means that Christ gives us, his grace and his love, and the handing over of our lives.

In the ancient world, those who had absolutely no resources at all had but one means left of ensuring that they could survive, to sell themselves into slavery. Christ is saying to the Laodiceans that they should become his slaves and he will heal them, sort out their destitution, and set them up in a healthy and fit way. At that time, in places where there were kings, their subjects were often their slaves. Thus, for many people the choice, if they had one, was of whom to serve, rather than whether to serve.

The 1776 Declaration of Independence by the 13 colonies that would become the United States of America was revolutionary, not merely in throwing off the authority of King George III, but also because it talked of the right of every human being (or at least, at the time, of every white male human being) to 'Life, Liberty and the pursuit of Happiness'. That breathtaking sentence, which has echoed around the world ever since, promotes the idea of autonomy, of being in charge of ourselves. Yet personal autonomy is an impossibility that conceals the enthroning of Mammon. In personal terms, autonomy assumes its own slavery – slavery to Mammon. The slavery may not be political, but it is moral and ethical as well as personal. In this passage in Revelation, Christ calls on the Laodiceans to see their real slavery, and to trade it for slavery to the one who brings true freedom.

The passage goes on to be increasingly positive. Jesus says that he disciplines those he loves, and therefore they should repent. He says that he stands at the door and knocks, and if they let him in, they will find that he sits and eats with them. Once again the words 'Eat with' do not do justice to the strength of the word used by John. The sense is of a leisurely, enjoyable time of fellowship, a feast of good company, a strengthening not only of body but also of mind, spirit and soul. This is the Christ who draws near to us and transforms our lives so completely that we become unrecognisable from the person we were before.

The passage ends with the promise that those who conquer will share the throne with Christ, in the same way as he himself conquered and sits down with his Father on his throne. When we dethrone Mammon and enthrone Christ, we do not find ourselves serving another tyrant but are ourselves invited to sit with Christ and to share his throne. The seat of the Archbishop of Canterbury in Canterbury Cathedral is very wide, enough for more than one person. In the stained glass of the cathedral, which is late medieval, the thrones of kings are always portrayed as very large, with the kings lounging across them. I never understood this, wondering if my predecessors in Augustine's Seat were much bigger than I am, until someone explained that, as a mark of honour, kings would invite people to sit with them on their throne. Dethroning Mammon is not a grim commitment to austerity and grey asceticism, but leads to joy, to mastery and to celebration.

These verses in Revelation 3 link into another extraordinary passage in Revelation 18. Much later in the book, this approaches the culmination of the whole biblical story as the New Jerusalem, the City of God, descends from heaven. The New Jerusalem is a depiction of heaven, in which God's just and gentle rule is established in every corner of creation. It is a picture of the ultimate urban regeneration, in which the city that is full of sin is replaced by the city that is full of God.

Revelation 18 marks the end of the city of sin. In this chapter, the city of sin is called Babylon. It is described as a place full of the wealthy, of merchants. It is the place to which every trader on earth goes, and where all those who have enthroned Mammon seek to belong. It is the commercial hub of the world.

REVELATION 18

After this I saw another angel coming down from heaven, having great authority; and the earth was made bright with his splendour. [2]He called out with a mighty voice,
'Fallen, fallen is Babylon the great!

It has become a dwelling place of demons,
a haunt of every foul spirit,

a haunt of every foul bird,

a haunt of every foul and hateful beast.
[3]For all the nations have drunk
of the wine of the wrath of her fornication,
and the kings of the earth have committed fornication
with her,
and the merchants of the earth have grown rich from the
power of her luxury.'
[4]Then I heard another voice from heaven saying,
'Come out of her, my people,

so that you do not take part in her sins,
and so that you do not share in her plagues;
[5]for her sins are heaped high as heaven,

and God has remembered her iniquities.
[6]Render to her as she herself has rendered,

and repay her double for her deeds;

mix a double draught for her in the cup she mixed.
[7]As she glorified herself and lived luxuriously,

so give her a like measure of torment and grief.
Since in her heart she says,

'I rule as a queen;
I am no widow,

and I will never see grief,'
    [8]therefore her plagues will come in a single day –
        pestilence and mourning and famine –
and she will be burned with fire;
        for mighty is the Lord God who judges her.'
    [9]And the kings of the earth, who committed fornication and lived in luxury with her, will weep and wail over her when they see the smoke of her burning; [10] they will stand far off, in fear of her torment, and say,
    'Alas, alas, the great city,
        Babylon, the mighty city!
For in one hour your judgment has come.'
    [11]And the merchants of the earth weep and mourn for her, since no one buys their cargo anymore, [12] cargo of gold, silver, jewels and pearls, fine linen, purple, silk and scarlet, all kinds of scented wood, all articles of ivory, all articles of costly wood, bronze, iron, and marble, [13]cinnamon, spice, incense, myrrh, frankincense, wine, olive oil, choice flour and wheat, cattle and sheep, horses and chariots, slaves – and human lives.
    [14]'The fruit for which your soul longed
        has gone from you,
and all your dainties and your splendour
        are lost to you,
never to be found again!'
    [15]The merchants of these wares, who gained wealth from her, will stand far off, in fear of her torment, weeping and mourning aloud,
    [16]'Alas, alas, the great city,
        clothed in fine linen,

in purple and scarlet,

adorned with gold,

with jewels, and with pearls!

[17]For in one hour all this wealth has been laid waste!'

And all shipmasters and seafarers, sailors and all whose trade is on the sea, stood far off [18]and cried out as they saw the smoke of her burning,

'What city was like the great city?'

[19]And they threw dust on their heads, as they wept and mourned, crying out,

'Alas, alas, the great city,

where all who had ships at sea

grew rich by her wealth!

For in one hour she has been laid waste.'

[20]Rejoice over her, O heaven, you saints and apostles and prophets! For God has given judgment for you against her.

[21]Then a mighty angel took up a stone like a great millstone and threw it into the sea, saying,

'With such violence Babylon the great city

will be thrown down,

and will be found no more;

[22]and the sound of harpists and minstrels and of flutists and trumpeters

will be heard in you no more;

and an artisan of any trade

will be found in you no more;

and the sound of the millstone

will be heard in you no more;

[23]and the light of a lamp

will shine in you no more;

> and the voice of bridegroom and bride
>   will be heard in you no more;
> for your merchants were the magnates of the earth,
>   and all nations were deceived by your sorcery.
> [24]And in you was found the blood of prophets and of saints,
>   and of all who have been slaughtered on earth.'

This 'capital of capitalism' is named Babylon because of that city's legendary riches, which go back to the era of its empire and its famous hanging gardens. In the Old Testament book of Daniel, King Nebuchadnezzar becomes so proud of this city – his city – that he is judged by God, and spends some years out of his mind living as a wild animal before being restored to full health. In Revelation, it is the city that stands for everything that opposes God. In 18:2, it is described as 'Babylon the Great', a city so powerful that it was unimaginable that it should ever fall – and yet the same verse says, 'Fallen, fallen is Babylon the Great!'

One of the deceits of Mammon is to pretend to everlasting life and eternal greatness. The book of Revelation exposes this as a fallacy. It is a theme that runs right through the Bible. In Isaiah, there is judgement against the wealthy of Israel, who pile up houses one after the other. Jeremiah and Ezekiel foretell the downfall of the wealthy. Daniel sees and names the illusion of Babylon. The preacher in Ecclesiastes speaks of the inability of any human being to ensure that the wealth that they have tried so hard to pile up will last.

A counter-narrative also runs through the Bible. Abraham is consoled by God's promise of faithfulness, to know that what he has been given by God will not disappear from his family. David is promised an eternal kingdom through his descendants, fulfilled in the person of Jesus Christ. Job is restored to wealth after his great suffering. Wealth is not of itself seen as evil in the Bible. Its malicious power is confined to the times in which it sits in power over us, rather than in service to us.

In Revelation 18, the fall of Babylon causes immense grief for all those who have shared in her wealth and enjoyed her benefits. Her fall is a result of the judgement of God. All those who have participated in the evil and 'lived in luxury with her, will weep and wail over her when they see the smoke of her burning' (v. 9).

In particular, in vv. 11-13, the trade of Babylon is described. In most respects it is similar to the kind of trading that goes on in many of our financial markets today, but ultimately it promises only destruction and despair. Revelation 18:17-18 says, "'For in one hour all this wealth has been laid waste!" And all shipmasters and seafarers, sailors and all whose trade is on the sea, stood far off and cried out as they saw the smoke of her burning, "What city was like the great city?"' Mammon is a deceiver, and those who are caught up by him will be betrayed by his deceit and end in despair.

These two passages in Revelation demonstrate why it is necessary to hold different emphases within Scripture in tension, and to hold them together so that one complements and balances the other. It is also an illustration of why context matters. Chapters 19-21 become more and more joyful. In

Revelation 19, the fall of Babylon is celebrated as the justice of God, and the rule of God is proclaimed in rejoicing throughout heaven and in unutterable joy. It almost immediately leads to the establishment of God's justice, and the overthrow of the devil and all his works. In Revelation 21, there is a new heaven and a new earth and the Holy City, the New Jerusalem, comes down out of heaven from God. The mastering of Babylon makes room for the rejoicing of heaven, and the regeneration of all that it is to be human and to live in God's creation. The dethroning of Mammon leads to liberty.

But how? How do we manage to ensure that Mammon is dethroned, and Christ takes his place in our society and in our lives? How can we find this place that is so abundant and hospitable that we are invited to be there with him?

The answer comes in two parts, one about us as individuals and one about the way in which we are called to be salt and light as God's people in the society in which we live.

First of all, as individuals we need to *listen*. Most of us – at least, most of us who would be willing to read a book like this – are unlikely to be consciously seeking to serve Mammon. We want our lives to be shaped by the values of Christ, which is why we take Lent seriously in preparation for Holy Week and Easter. We seek to shape our lives in a way that we have already examined earlier in this book, and not to be deceived by what we find around us.

Yet the letter to Laodicea sounds a warning. The deception of Mammon is endless, and like winter colds in England, comes around continually. We have no sooner got rid of it in one place, than it seeks to creep in elsewhere. The Laodiceans thought they had things pretty well squared off, but they were

completely wrong. The last sentence of each of the letters to
the seven churches is, 'Let those who have ears listen to what
the Spirit says to the churches.'

We dethrone by listening. Then we enthrone Christ by
listening – and acting.

We must be sure that we see the world as it is, and the only
way to do so is to see it through God's eyes. This is a problem
that every Christian has always faced, and always will.

Who are the people in your life that you talk to about money?
Think about how you can build relationships of trust
with them so that you can be open and accountable.

It is why Saint Ignatius of Loyola, the founder of the Jesuits,
created his spiritual exercises, which are above all a path
towards greater self-awareness and greater stability in
Christian service and life. They recognise the moments
of consolation and desolation, and our vulnerability when
we find ourselves in the latter. They recognise that mood,
health and circumstances can all lead us to be spiritually
blind, like the Laodiceans. The answer has to be in constant
re-engagement, and regular periods of deep self-reflection,
ideally with others whose love is so sure that we can listen
to criticism without being knocked sideways by it. I am
fortunate enough to work with some such people, and the
benefit to me has been immeasurable. I owe them more
than I can say.

Second, as individuals we need to *repent*. We cannot only
see, but we must act. Repentance means stopping, turning

around and going in the opposite direction. In terms of dethroning Mammon, repentance will be seen in reviewing our giving, in reviewing our spending and in reviewing the whole way we accumulate our wealth. What do we want wealth for? How is it speaking to us? Is it telling us that so long as we have it, we are safe, and therefore we must hold on to it whatever happens? Is it telling us that the amount we have reflects our true value in the world, and our true security for the future? Repentance is about answering those questions in a new and different way.

We *listen*, then we *repent*. The third part of our personal response is to *enthrone Christ* in Mammon's place. To enthrone is to surrender authority, as the Laodiceans were called to do, so that we have a new ruler in our lives. We need to accept (and this is the work of a lifetime) the value that Christ sets on us, taking him at his word that we are of infinite worth and deeply loved. We need to spend time in celebration and rejoicing at the grace that he has given us, so that its reality is more and more established in our lives. The result according to the testimonies of Christians throughout the ages, in places of plenty and of want, in times of security and of fear, has been liberation and joy. Cardinal Văn Thuận, alone in his cell, celebrating the mass with his one grain of rice and enough rice wine to hold in the palm of his hand, spoke of the joy he found in Christ. When I met him, and listened to a conversation between him and a friend of mine, it was not about themselves and their lives, or the political ups and downs of church and state. The only thing that really interested them was the joy of prayer and communion with Christ. It is one of the most precious conversations that I have ever heard.

But we mustn't feel that we need to dethrone Mammon all by ourselves. Revelation 18 demonstrates that God does that very adequately. Our role as individuals is to be people who, through our repentance, have enthroned Christ. In the same way as darkness cannot live in the presence of light, so Mammon cannot rule in the presence of Christ. Enthrone Christ and be willing to let finance be transformed in your own life and that of family and home, and let God take care of Mammon.

Are there things in your life that you need to surrender in order to allow Jesus Christ to be the ruler of your life?

Beyond the personal level, there is much more to dethroning Mammon and enthroning Christ. It has always been one of the faults of Protestant Christianity that we see virtue too often in purely personal terms, and forget that almost everything that happens in the New Testament is addressed to communities and to churches and to groups, and even to societies and nations. This is particularly true of the book of Revelation.

What does a society look like in which Christ is enthroned and Mammon is dethroned? We need not be too pessimistic. In many ways, especially in Britain in the post-Second World War era, that is very much what has happened. Those who, in the late 1940s and in subsequent governments, sought to ensure that every sick person would have free medical treatment, that every child would have an education, that every person in poverty would be given a sufficiency with which to combat the extremes of poverty and hunger, were enthroning Christ over Mammon, whether or not they knew it. And for many of them this was their conscious motivation – especially for William Beveridge. The impetus he was given by the writings and leadership of my predecessor Archbishop William Temple, and by the political philosophy of R. H. Tawney, set a lasting template for what was seen not merely as acceptable but as right in society.

It was also visible in the nineteenth century. There was similar progress, in the 1830s and 1840s, and throughout the nineteenth and twentieth centuries, with the establishment of the Factory Acts, the beginnings of health and safety at work legislation, and limitations on working hours and the use, first of children, then women, then eventually men, in conditions that were either dangerous or insufferably terrible. That trend continues today. Even in the last 30 years, conditions at work have improved immeasurably.

What aspects of community life are you thankful for?
What aspects are you passionate about maintaining? Or adding?
Which aspects of your community restrict the flourishing of human beings within it?
What might it involve for you to work to dethrone Mammon in those parts of your community?

Yet, as we have seen, Cony and Fin, those two disciples of Mammon, continue to weave their spells around the experience and lives of many people. They set government policy, and encourage contempt for those without means

who are caught in poverty. They blind the eyes of those who
follow them, so that their acolytes think that someone who
is not rich is either stupid or lacking in drive. One piece
of evidence on the Parliamentary Commission on Banking
Standards, of which I was a member, related to the PPI
scandal – the selling of insurance by some banks. This was
often embedded in the cost of loans, which made the banks
a great deal of money and gave no realistic protection to
those to whom it applied. One person giving evidence, who
had been in a leading position in one of the banks involved,
robustly refuted the idea that the kind of bonuses that were
paid to those who sold the insurance (often not understanding the fallacy of what they were doing) could have
been an inducement to wrongdoing. He made the point that
they earned very little, so a 10 per cent bonus would only
be worth £1,500 or £2,000. He could not grasp the idea
that for someone earning £15,000 to £20,000 each year,
with a family to feed and bills to pay, a bonus of that size
could make all the difference, particularly at a time when
higher interest rates were making mortgage repayments
more costly. It would be of infinitely greater worth than the
value of the bonuses 100 times bigger earned by those at
the top of the tree.

There may be some rhetorical value in an archbishop calling on society to repent of its view of Mammon. But I am not
convinced that – beyond a few passing news headlines – it
will have a great deal of lasting impact. However, the lessons
of history demonstrate the capacity of a group within society
to change attitudes, and I dream that we – as the Church –
might rise to the call to be that group.

Let us look at a few examples. Some of them are about political pressure, and others are about consumer choices.

One of them has already been mentioned. The UK's commitment of 0.7 per cent of national income to the aid budget is one that springs out of long campaigning by groups – Christian and otherwise – with a deep concern about global poverty. It has become established policy, despite attacks from many quarters, and is something that we can continue to speak in favour of, supporting those politicians who defend it – often against their own political interests – so that, over time, the sense that it marks a point of virtue in our society becomes more deeply established.

The use of social security benefits – currently in the midst of a huge upheaval and reform, the long-term effect of which has yet to be seen – is also something about which we should not remain silent. Many groups, including the churches, have spoken powerfully about the need to improve the current policy around so-called 'benefit sanctions'. This involves the withholding of social security benefits for a period if the person receiving them is deemed not to be actively seeking work. But such policies must respect dignity and encourage good human behaviour. A system that encourages you to serve your own interest, regardless of what is happening around you, is not something to be admired or advocated. The incentives of the tax and benefits systems must not shy away from being consciously virtuous. Neither system is morally neutral, but both encourage certain types of behaviours that must be held in balance.

There is currently – and rightly – much pressure to reform the tax system, both in the UK and globally. Its complexity has grown inexorably over time, so that, in many companies and for many rich individuals, tax planning overwhelms strategic development. I witnessed this in my earlier career, where good decisions were often challenged by the tax department because they reduced the efficiency of tax planning. It is easy to be negative about companies and claim that they are not doing their duty. We need to say positively what tax should do for human flourishing, and to say it in a way that enables policy to be decided simply and clearly. We can challenge this language of tax 'liabilities', dethroning Mammon by saying that the ultimate aim of taxation is to provide money to enable the state to ensure the dignity, safety, health and education of all citizens, which guarantees our common good, and allows us to show solidarity abroad.

Are you proud to pay tax?
Would you pay it even if no-one was looking?

Perhaps the churches' finest hour in dethroning Mammon in recent years has been Church support for Jubilee 2000. Jubilee 2000 was an international coalition movement involving over forty countries globally, calling for the cancellation of debt in the world's poorest countries by the year 2000. Mammon wanted his due, but impoverished nations were bankrupting themselves servicing interest payments on debts long since repaid. Sustained support from Christians and others across the world ultimately led to the cancellation of more than $100 billion of debt owed by thirty-five of the poorest countries.

Started in the UK in the 1970s by students from Durham, an example of listening, repenting and enthroning is the fair trade movement. By 1998, the fair trade market in the UK was worth around £17 million annually. Now this market is worth over £1 billion a year. In coffee alone, almost a quarter of the UK's roast and ground market now carries the Fairtrade mark. Fairtrade bananas were introduced in 1996 and now a third of all the bananas we buy are Fairtrade. In the UK, we eat 3,000 Fairtrade bananas every minute! We already have a track record at playing Mammon at his own game, and defeating him by enthroning Christ in our decisions at the checkout.

How proud are you of the spending decisions you make
at the checkout or online?
How are you using your spending power to enthrone Christ in the
economy around you?

Some may be aware that a key focus of mine has been consumer debt. In 2014, I launched a Task Group on Responsible Credit and Savings. The aim was to create a fairer financial system, one that focused on serving the whole community, where everyone has access to responsible credit and savings – a system that enthrones Christ and not Mammon. This work is now being carried forward by the Just Finance Foundation, set up especially to continue the work of the Task Group. Through the programmes that the Task Group instigated, thousands of children are now involved in LifeSavers, a financial education programme in primary schools and, through local churches, people are being trained as Credit Champions, signposting people in their communities towards the right products and services for them.

The churches, among other groups, had already been attentive to this growing concern and, to highlight the commitment of churches to modelling better systems, the Churches Mutual Credit Union was established, a collaboration between the Church of England, the Church of Scotland, the Scottish Episcopal Church, the Methodist Church of Great Britain and the Church in Wales. From a standing start, it already has over six hundred members and assets of £1.4 million, which can be used for low-interest loans and helps people to develop a culture of saving. More generally in the UK, membership of credit unions has grown by 123,000 (or 13 per cent) since July 2013, and credit union assets grew by 21 per cent over the same period. At the same time, the volume of payday lending in the UK has declined by 68 per cent from its peak in 2013, and Citizens Advice reports a 53 per cent drop in the number of payday loan problems they helped with between April and June 2015 compared to the same period in 2014. We can make a difference.

Our list could go on but one thing is essential. The Church should be deeply involved in speaking into society, not because it is always right or has perfect wisdom – far from it! – but because it dances to a different tune and sees a different vision. Because we have a different ruler on the throne.

Who is on the throne in your life: Mammon or Christ?
What might God be calling you to do next?

NOTES

INTRODUCTION

1   In referring to Mammon, Jesus personalises 'him' as a master (Matthew 6:24). Although I am generally keen to resist using *male* language as a default setting, I have chosen to continue to refer to Mammon as 'he' and 'him' in most parts of this book. To introduce the female pronoun is not helpful here; while the idea of dethroning an 'it' makes no sense at all.

2   Y. Varoufakis, *And the Weak Suffer What They Must? Europe, Austerity and the Threat to Global Stability* (London: Bodley Head, 2016).

3   For a wonderful and passionate account of this, see Robert Skidelsky, *John Maynard Keynes: Fighting for Britain 1937–1946* (London: MacMillan, 2000), Parts Two and Three, pp. 179ff.

CHAPTER 1

1   According to a 2015 OECD report, 'In most countries, the gap between rich and poor is at its highest level since 30 years. Today, in OECD countries [which includes the UK], the richest 10 per cent of the population earn 9.6 times the income of the poorest 10 per cent. In the 1980s, this ratio stood at 7:1 rising to 8:1 in the 1990s and 9:1 in the 2000s.' (Source: OECD, *In It Together: Why Less Inequality Benefits All*, OECD Publishing, 2015).

CHAPTER 2

1 The quotation is taken from the Anglican Communion Environmental Network (ACEN) Declaration of Good Friday 2015.

2 Beatty, C. & Fothergill, S. (2016) 'The uneven impact of welfare reform: the financial losses to places and people'. Centre for Regional Economic and Social Research, Sheffield Hallam University, p. 3.

3 *The Rule of Benedict* (Harmondsworth: Penguin Classics, 2008).

4 N. Stern, *Why Are We Waiting? The Logic, Urgency, and Promise of Tackling Climate Change* (London: The MIT Press, 2015), pp. 146–7.

CHAPTER 3

1 I refer back to Matthew 13:45-6, explored in the Introduction, pp. 2–4.

2 I draw here on some words sent to me by Zac Koons, communicating on ideas inspired by Sam Wells. See Samuel Wells, *Be Not Afraid* (Grand Rapids, MI: Brazos Press, 2011) and *Learning to Dream Again* (Norwich: Canterbury Press, 2013).

3 I am borrowing this term from Ched Myers of Bartimaeus Cooperative Ministries. See his *The Biblical Vision of Sabbath Economics* (published by *Tell the Word*, a project of Church of the Saviour, Massachusetts).

4 See, for example, Ecclesiastes 3:1-14 and 4:13-16. Also 5:10-11 and 6:7-9.

5 As a number of my eagle-eyed colleagues have pointed out, to be grammatically correct the slogan should have been 'More parties, *fewer* meetings'. It should, but it wasn't. My sloganeering is a pedantry-free zone. 'All power to the people through the Bolsheviks' lacked syntactical elegance but overthrew an empire. It is, of course, better in Russian.

CHAPTER 4

1   D. Kahneman and A. Deaton, 'High Income Improves Evaluation of Life but Not Emotional Well-being', *Proceedings of the National Academy of Science*, 2010, 107 (38): 16489–93.

CHAPTER 5

1   See, for example, P. Ricoeur, 'Ethical and Theological Considerations on the Golden Rule', in *Figuring the Sacred: Religion, Narrative, and Imagination* (Minneapolis: Augsburg Fortress, 1995), pp. 293–302.

2   P. H. Dembinski, *Finance: Servant or Deceiver? Financialization at the Crossroads* (Basingstoke, Palgrave Macmillan, 2009), p. 98.

CHAPTER 6

1   Two such examples would be the radical reformers in Münster during the Reformation, or the Diggers and the Levellers during the English Civil War (1642-51).

2   J. Mayer, *Dark Money: The Hidden History of the Billionaires Behind the Rise of the Radical Right* (Kindle Edition, Doubleday Books, 2016), location 779.

3   Ibid., location 23.

4   J. Kovacs and C. Rowland, *Revelation: The Apocalypse of Jesus Christ* (Oxford: Wiley-Blackwell Bible Commentaries, 2004), p. 52.

ACKNOWLEDGEMENTS

In writing this book, I have relied very heavily on many people, a few of whom I want to thank by name. Particular thanks must go to Jo Bailey Wells, until 2016 my Chaplain and now Bishop of Dorking. Her encouragement and guidance have been wonderful. Hiding far away in Austin, Texas, has been Zac Koons, who offered significant scriptural research, and has made many helpful additions and corrections. My colleagues Jack Palmer-White and Jess Wyatt have worked with immense patience, often asking, 'Yes, but what does that mean?' in response to my meandering prose. They have also assisted in drawing together the research that has gone into this book. Emma Shelton, new to the team here, found one of her first duties was to transcribe the entire first draft from a dictating machine. She has my sympathy and admiration, for her resolute cheerfulness. The theological retreat group I meet with twice a year, convened by Professor David Ford, have helped enormously, not least because they know far more than I do. Eve Poole, Jeremy Anderson and Sam Wells provided helpful advice at the final hurdle. Many others have also helped wittingly or unwittingly, including Mark Carney, Ken Costa, Philip Mountstephen, Paul Perkin, Phil Simpson, Andy Wheeler, former colleagues at Enterprise Oil and Elf Aquitaine, especially Sir Graham Hearne, John

Walmsley, Julian West and André Gester, and more others than I can remember.

I am especially grateful to Bloomsbury, their editors, and to Caroline Chartres, for her encouragement.

Then, of course, I want to say something about my family. The insanity of taking on this task, as a non-academic with no writing experience, on top of a somewhat demanding day job, has added to the stress they carry on my behalf. They are wonderful in every way.

Finally, I want to voice a loud disclaimer. I am neither a professional economist nor a professional theologian. I am more than aware of the weaknesses of this book. On some days I have felt that the only reason for continuing was – as they used to say on the BBC show *Mastermind* – 'I've started so I'll finish.' The many faults are mine. Anything useful is grace, and grace operating through those I have mentioned above.

INDEX